Lemon v. Kurtzman and the Separation of Church and State Debate

Debating Supreme Court Decisions

Kathiann M. Kowalski

Enslow Publishers, Inc.

40 Industrial Road   PO Box 38
Box 398   Aldershot
Berkeley Heights, NJ 07922   Hants GU12 6BP
USA   UK
http://www.enslow.com

This book is dedicated to my husband, Michael Meissner.

Copyright © 2005 by Kathiann M. Kowalski

Library of Congress Cataloging-in-Publication Data

Kowalski, Kathiann M., 1955-
Lemon v. Kurtzman and the separation of church and state debate : debating
Supreme Court decisions / Kathiann M. Kowalski.— 1st ed.
    p. cm. — (Debating Supreme Court decisions)
Includes bibliographical references and index.
ISBN 0-7660-2391-5
    1. Lemon, Alton—Trials, litigation, etc.—Juvenile literature. 2. Pennsylvania—
Trials, litigation, etc.—Juvenile literature. 3. Education—Finance—Law and
legislation—Pennsylvania—Juvenile literature. 4. Church and state—United States—
Juvenile literature. I. Title: Lemon versus Kurtzman and the separation of church
and state debate. II. Title. III. Series.
KF228.L46K69 2005
342.7308'52—dc22

                                                    2004020156

Printed in the United States of America

10 9 8 7 6 5 4 3 2 1

To Our Readers: We have done our best to make sure that all Internet Addresses in this
book were active and appropriate when we went to press. However, the author and publisher
have no control over and assume no liability for the material available on those Internet sites
or on other Web sites they may link to. Any comments or suggestions can be sent by e-mail
to comments@enslow.com or to the address on the back cover.

Illustration Credits: All photos are from AP/Wide World except for the
following: Hemera Image Express, p. 2.

Cover Illustration: Background, Artville; photographs, Photos.com (left), Corel
Corp. (right).

Contents

Acknowledgments

The author gratefully thanks the following people for sharing their insights and offering other help: Derek Davis, J. M. Dawson Institute of Church-State Studies, Baylor University; Ronald B. Flowers, Texas Christian University; Steven Freeman and Todd Gutnick, Anti-Defamation League; Jeremy Leaming, Americans United for Separation of Church and State; John W. Whitehead and Nisha Mohammed, The Rutherford Institute. The author also benefited from the scholarship and teaching of her former professors on constitutional law topics, including Albert Sacks, Milton Katz, and Stephen Breyer at the Harvard Law School, and Howard Ball at Hofstra University. Last but not least, she thanks her husband, Michael Meissner, and their children, Chris, Laura, and Bethany, for their encouragement and support.

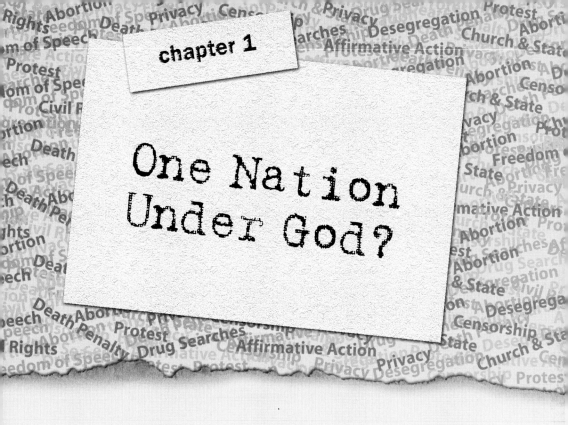

One Nation Under God?

"I pledge allegiance to the flag of the United States of America. . . ."

Across America, children start the school day with the Pledge of Allegiance. People say the pledge at many public events too.

In 2002, a federal appeals court shocked the country. The court said the pledge's words were unconstitutional—at least in public schools. The problem was one phrase: "under God."

In the court's view, those words went against the First Amendment. Among other things, that part of the Constitution deals with religion and government.

People have said the pledge that way for about fifty years. But in the United States, a law that goes against the Constitution cannot stand. It makes no difference how long people have done it.

Challenging the Pledge of Allegiance

Michael Newdow was a single father living in Sacramento, California. His second-grade daughter lived with her mom, whom Newdow had never married. The girl went to public school in California. State law called for students to say the Pledge of Allegiance every school day.

Newdow is an atheist. He does not believe in God. While he works as a doctor, he also has a law degree. Newdow filed the lawsuit *pro se*, or on his own. He challenged the pledge under the First Amendment. The First Amendment says:

> Congress shall make no law respecting an establishment of religion, or prohibiting the free exercise thereof; or abridging the freedom of speech, or of the press; or the right of the people peaceably to assemble, and to petition the Government for a redress of grievances.

The district court dismissed Newdow's case. He appealed to the Ninth Circuit Court of Appeals, which reversed the district court's decision. By a two to one vote, the three-judge panel said the words "under God" were unconstitutional.

A clergyman wrote the Pledge of Allegiance in 1892. Congress adopted it by law in 1942. At that time, America was fighting World War II. The pledge showed public loyalty to the United States.

Congress added the words "under God" in 1954. The United States and the Soviet Union were in the Cold War. Actual war did not break out between them, but tensions ran high. The communist-run Soviet Union did not allow any dissent. It did not allow freedom of the speech or press. Churches could not operate freely.

Many people in America feared the "godless communists." They felt proud of America's religious heritage. What better way to celebrate this, they thought, than by declaring the country "one nation under God"?

"The children of our land, in the daily recitation of the pledge in school, will be daily impressed with a true understanding of our way of life and its origins," said Louis Rabaut.[1] He sponsored the 1954 law in the House of Representatives. Congress passed the bill, and President Dwight Eisenhower signed it into law. The president said:

> From this day forward, the millions of our school children will daily proclaim in every city and town, every village and rural schoolhouse, the dedication of our Nation and our people to the Almighty.[2]

The state, school board, and federal government felt Newdow had no right to complain. The law called for schools to say the Pledge of

Allegiance each day. But children did not have to take part if it went against their religious beliefs. Also, other aspects of public life have references to God. Newdow might not believe in God, but millions of other Americans do. To them, the pledge describes American life and its freedom. Why couldn't Newdow just respect that?

Two of the three judges sided with Newdow. They felt the purpose of the 1954 law was to advance religion. They said the law made people who did not believe in God feel like outsiders. Especially for schoolchildren, the court said, hearing the pledge with the words "under God" was coercive, or intimidating. Children would feel the school approved of some beliefs, but not others.[3]

Judge Ferdinand Fernandez disagreed. He felt any religious effect was *de minimis*. That means something is so tiny that it does not matter. Besides, if "one nation under God" was not allowed, what was next? Should the word "God" come out of patriotic songs? Should it come off all money? In the judge's view, that would rob people of "the awe we all must feel at the immenseness of the universe and our own small place within it, as well as the wonder we must feel at the good fortune of our country."[4]

Both the majority and the dissent cited a 1943 case, *West Virginia State Board of Education v.*

Legal Terms

amicus curiae—Literally, "friend of the court;" someone who files a brief in a case her or she is not a party, but has a strong interest. Such briefs let the court benefit from the added viewpoint.

appellate court (also called court of appeals)—A court that reviews decisions of lower courts for fairness and accuracy. An appellate court can reverse a lower court's ruling.

appellant—The person who feels the lower court made an error.

appellee—The person who won the case in the lower court.

brief—Written statement of a party's argument on one or more issues in the case.

concur—To agree with the majority in a court case.

dicta—Extra comments in a legal opinion in addition to the case's holding; nonbinding statements of a judge's views in a legal opinion.

dissent—To disagree with the majority in a court case.

majority opinion—The ruling and reasoning supported by a majority of appellate court judges in a case. **Concurring opinions** are written by judges who agree with the majority opinion but have other reasons for their views. **Dissenting opinions** are written by judges who disagree with the ruling.

precedent—A legal holding that will determine how courts decide future cases.

Barnette.[5] Members of the Jehovah's Witnesses sued in that case. Their faith would not let them pledge allegiance to anyone but God. The Supreme Court had ruled against them in an earlier case. Now it agreed that no one had to say the pledge if it went against their conscience. Later cases said schools could not even force children to stand at attention during the pledge.[6]

Barnette dealt with the Jehovah's Witnesses' freedom to practice their religion. But the Supreme Court did not make everyone stop saying the pledge. It just said the children with religious objections did not have to say it.

In the *Newdow* case, the Ninth Circuit said atheist children could feel coerced just by hearing the words "under God." But Jehovah's Witness children still hear other people say the pledge. Why shouldn't that be enough for atheist children too? The dissent suggested this point.

The pledge case sparked public outcry. In Washington, D.C., members of Congress gathered on the steps of the Capitol. Together they said the Pledge of Allegiance—with the words "under God." A few months later, they passed a law stating their view that the text of the pledge should stay that way.[7]

A full panel of the Ninth Circuit's judges could have reversed the decision. Nine judges wanted to do that. The other fifteen sided with Newdow. With a minor change, the court's initial opinion stood.[8]

The Ninth Circuit covers California and other western states. In early 2003, 9.6 million children in those areas started saying the pledge without the words "under God."[9]

Ten years before the *Newdow* case, the Seventh Circuit Court of Appeals reached the opposite result in a similar case. In *Sherman* v. *Community Consolidated School District 21*, it held that saying the pledge in schools with the words "under God" was not an establishment of religion.[10] The Seventh Circuit covers Illinois, Indiana, and Wisconsin.

Now two federal courts of appeal had conflicting rulings. If *Newdow* stood, people in different states would say different versions of the pledge. In October 2003, the Supreme Court said it would hear the case.

In March 2004, Newdow argued before the Supreme Court. Three months later, the Supreme Court reversed the Ninth Circuit.

Justice John Paul Stevens wrote the Court's opinion, in which four other Justices joined. In the majority's view, Newdow lacked standing. In other words, he did not have a legal right to bring his claim before the Court. In particular, a state court custody order gave the mother final say on matters

Middle school students in Florida say the Pledge of Allegiance. The Supreme Court would be asked to consider whether the words "under God" should be removed from the pledge.

affecting the child. The mother wanted her Christian daughter to say the pledge.

Based on this, a majority felt the Court should not rule on the merits of the case.[11] The Court reversed the Ninth Circuit's ruling. But it did not rule on the basic question of whether the words "under God" violate the First Amendment.

Justices William Rehnquist, Sandra Day O'Connor, and Clarence Thomas disagreed with the majority on the issue of standing. Newdow was the girl's natural father. They felt he had a right to bring his claim to court. But they disagreed with Newdow on the constitutional question. In their view, saying the Pledge of Allegiance in school did not violate the First Amendment.[12]

Newdow lost his case, but the Supreme Court still has not made a definitive ruling on the pledge's words. The underlying question, and many other issues about church and state, remain open to debate.

Tension in the First Amendment

Two parts of the First Amendment deal with religion. The Establishment Clause says there shall be "no law respecting an establishment of religion." The Free Exercise Clause forbids any law "prohibiting the free exercise" of religion.

This book deals with the Establishment Clause. Practically everyone agrees that the United States may not have an official religion without violating the Constitution. Historically, many countries had official religions. In colonial times, for example, the Roman Catholic Church was the official church in France. The Church of England, or Anglican Church, was the official church in England.

Even now, some countries have official religions. In some cases, people may suffer discrimination if they do not belong to that faith. In other cases, a government may give money or other support to the official religion, but still let people practice other faiths.

The Church of England is still the established

church in the United Kingdom. The Church of Scotland, which is Presbyterian, is also an official church there. Norway's official church is the Evangelical Lutheran Church. In each of these cases, the established churches get support from the government. But people may follow other faiths if they choose.

Saudi Arabia's official religion is Wahhabism, a branch of Sunni Islam. Followers actively encourage their neighbors to follow what they believe to be God's laws. Thus, a religious police force, the *mutawwiin*, enforces standards on dress, conduct of business, and so forth. In Iran, Shiah Islam is the official state religion. The minority there who practice the Baha'i faith suffer discrimination. Baha'is believe that God's word is revealed through a variety of prophets, and they favor equal roles in society for both sexes.

In the United States, the Establishment Clause does not mean just that there shall be no official church. Over time, the courts have said that government cannot favor any religion, promote religion in general, or get too tied up in religious issues. Most people in the United States would agree that the government should not favor one particular church. People differ more on whether government can promote religion in general. People also disagree on what constitutes too much government involvement in religious issues.

Even when they agree on general principles, Americans often differ on what to do in particular cases. Must every reference to God be cut out of public life? Can government aid to individuals indirectly help churches? When might such action cross the line into promoting religion?

As *Newdow* and *Barnette* show, the same government action that arguably establishes one religious view can also potentially threaten the free exercise of another religion. Newdow felt that saying "under God" in the pledge promoted belief in God, and thus violated the Establishment Clause. At the same time, he felt it interfered with atheists' right under the Free Exercise Clause to believe there is no God.

Other cases present tension between the First Amendment's two religion clauses. Some students may feel they have a right to include their religious views in original one-act plays for the school drama production. Other students may feel the school is endorsing those views if it lets the drama club produce the play. Both parts of the First Amendment state important rights. When they seem to collide, both sides feel they are right.

Why Does Separation of Church and State Matter Today?

America is a diverse country. It has over fifteen hundred different religious denominations. People worship at about 360,000 places.[13] There are churches, temples, mosques, synagogues, and more.

Many religions hold there is one God, although they may differ on who that is and how they worship. Christianity, Judaism, and Islam are examples. Some faiths, like Hinduism, involve belief in many gods. Other religious followers do not worship any god, but instead follow a philosophy of life. Confucianism and Buddhism are examples.

People also vary in how they practice religion. Some people go to formal worship services one or more times a week. Some go only on important religious holidays. Other people believe in a religion, but they do not belong to any particular church.

Still other people do not follow any religion. Some of them follow certain philosophies. Other people just do what they feel is right.

With so many different views, most Americans are glad for the Establishment Clause. At a minimum, it means the government cannot make someone follow any particular religion.

But disputes often arise about what the clause means. Newdow challenged the Pledge of Allegiance in public schools. Are any religious practices allowed in public schools? Does it matter who is the moving force behind such practices?

The United States has thousands of private

schools too. Religious groups run many of them. Can the government help those students? Where should one draw the line?

Beyond this, should mention of God be part of public events? Can religious symbols appear in public places? Do chaplains have any place in the military? When, if ever, should religious institutions get government money for social programs?

Over two hundred years have passed since the Constitution's ratification. Yet the Establishment Clause still raises questions.

As you read this book, reflect on your own views about religion. Many people are passionate about their beliefs. That colors their views on church and state.

"Both church and state call for our allegiance," notes Derek Davis at Baylor University's J. M. Dawson Institute of Church-State Studies.[14] That tension has posed problems throughout history. Many people want religious principles to guide their government. But sometimes people feel that church and state blend too much. Then they may worry about losing their freedom.

Keep in mind that people on both sides of a case believe they are right. Try to see the issues in this book from different sides. Think about how you would weigh different arguments if you were a judge. You may hold your own personal opinions and religious views. But judges must decide cases under applicable laws and the Constitution. The Constitution is the supreme law in the United States. As a legal matter, it takes priority over all other laws at the federal and state government levels. Ultimately, the First Amendment is intended to protect everyone in this country.

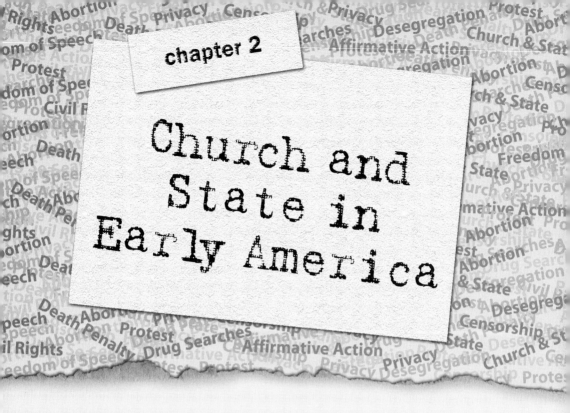

chapter 2

Church and State in Early America

Religion has always been important in America. But the roles of church and state have changed over time.

Religion in Early New England

The Pilgrims landed at Plymouth, Massachusetts, in 1620. They wanted to break away from the Church of England, or Anglican Church. English law forbade that. The group went to Holland for a while. Then they came to America. They could practice their faith freely here.

The Puritans started Massachusetts Bay Colony in 1630. They did not want to break away from the Anglican Church. They wanted to purify it from within. The group suffered persecution in England.

The Puritans had a theocracy, or church-led

government. They could practice their religion freely. But they did not give other people that freedom. They were afraid that other views could corrupt the colony.

Roger Williams felt that conscience was more important than what church leaders said. The Puritan leaders banished Williams. In 1636, he founded Providence, Rhode Island. He chose the name to honor God's merciful providence, which means guidance or care.

In 1644, Williams wrote about liberty of conscience. Separation of church and state was not just a good idea for government, he said; it was the best way to save one's soul too. Williams' words influenced later political thinkers.

The Puritans also banished Anne Hutchinson. She disagreed about the roles of good works and grace. Basically, the debate was about how important good works were to salvation. Did God's grace alone save someone from hell? Or did one also have to exert personal effort by helping others? Hutchinson criticized the ministers' sermons too. The Puritans forced her to leave. Hutchinson went to Rhode Island. Later, she moved to New York.

The Puritans also banished Hutchinson's friend Mary Dyer. Later, Dyer joined the Society of Friends, or Quakers. The religion was illegal in Massachusetts Bay Colony. Dyer went back anyway. In 1660, the Puritans hanged her.

The Salem witch trials of 1692 signaled the height of the Puritans' power. Teenage girls accused several people of witchcraft. The Puritans killed about twenty alleged witches. Only later did people see that the executions had gone too far. After that, the power of the Puritan ministers shrank.

Over time, the Puritan religion became the Congregational Church. It no longer had full control over government. Except for Rhode Island, it was the official religion in most New England colonies.

Maryland: A Temporary Haven for Catholics

Maryland began in 1634 as a place for Catholics to practice their faith freely. Yet in the early years, only one fourth of the people were Catholic. In 1645, Protestant groups led attacks of robbery, or plundering, against Catholics.

Afterward, the colony passed the Maryland Toleration Act. The 1649 law said,

> No person or persons whatsoever within this Province . . . professing to beleive [sic] in Jesus Christ, shall from henceforth be any waies troubled, molested or discountenanced for or in respect of his or her religion nor in the free exercise thereof. . . .[1]

The law was very limited. Its terms protected Christians only. But it was a step toward religious freedom.

Less than forty years later, though, Protestants took over. The Anglican Church became the official religion in 1692. Everyone paid taxes to support it.

Then a 1704 law closed all Catholic churches and schools. Maryland started as a "Catholic colony." It was not that any longer.

Pennsylvania: The Quaker Experiment

In 1681, William Penn started Pennsylvania as a proprietary colony, or business venture. Penn made money from farming, rents, and so on. But Penn also wanted his colony to be a "holy experiment."

Penn did not want any government religion—not even his own Quaker faith. Instead, the colony's charter guaranteed freedom of worship to all "who shall confess and acknowledge *One* almighty God."[2] While this still left out atheists and pagans, Jewish people would be free to practice their faith. Even so, only Christians could hold office.

Pennsylvania's religious freedom and economic opportunities attracted other Quakers. Catholics, Lutherans, and other Protestant groups went there too. By the 1770s, several hundred Jewish people lived there as well.

Other Colonies

New York began in 1624 as the Dutch colony of New Netherlands. The British took it over in 1664. The British did not outlaw the earlier colonists' Dutch Reformed Church. They let all Christians practice their religion.

Virginia and the Carolinas were started as proprietary colonies. Georgia began as a place for debtors to make a new start. These southern colonies had the Anglican Church as their official religion.

Gradually, people became more tolerant of other religions. During the Revolutionary War, members of different faiths fought side by side. Yet nine of the thirteen colonies still had official churches for all or part of their areas. Rhode Island, Delaware, Pennsylvania, and New Jersey were the exceptions.[3]

Making Rules for a New Country

During its first years, America was a confederation. Basically, it was a loose alliance of states. Under the Articles of Confederation, there was a central government, but it was very weak. The states held most of the power in the new country.

During this time, James Madison argued against letting the state of Virginia pay to support religious teachers. It was a matter of principle. To "force a citizen to contribute three pence only of his property for the support of any one establishment" was a denial of liberty.[4]

Thomas Jefferson did not want established churches either. In 1786, the state legislature passed the Virginia Bill for Religious Liberty, which he wrote. Jefferson saw it as one of his three greatest achievements—along with writing the Declaration of Independence and founding the University of Virginia. Later, in 1802, he would write that there should be a "wall of separation" between church and state.

America's weak central government had many problems. In 1787, the Constitutional Convention met in Philadelphia. The delegates wrote our Constitution.

Some states hesitated to ratify, or approve, the Constitution. They wanted guarantees for individual rights. They wanted to protect state rights too. In response, Congress proposed the amendments that became our Bill of Rights.

Congress looked at different ways to word the First Amendment's religion clauses. One idea was to forbid any "national religion." Another was to say no religion would get preference. Yet another idea was to add a clause on the right of conscience.[5]

Finally, the House and Senate Conference Committee agreed on language. Congress sent that wording to the states. They ratified it in 1791, and it became the First Amendment.

The United States' Early Years

Religion played a big part in American life. In his Farewell Address, President George Washington said:

> Of all the dispositions and habits which lead to political prosperity, religion and morality are indispensable supports. . . . reason and experience both forbid us to expect that national morality can prevail in exclusion of religious principle.[6]

In practice, states sometimes gave preferences to religions. For example, a 1785 North Carolina law let public money rebuild an old Episcopal church. Any Christian minister could then use it on Sundays. A 1790 Delaware law said only "ministers or preachers of the gospel" could marry people.[7] These laws helped Christian groups only.

In general, states viewed the First Amendment as binding upon the federal government. It was not until the twentieth century that the Supreme Court made clear that its religion clauses limit states' actions too. Even in the nineteenth century, however, various states were moving to "disestablish" religion at the state level. In other words, they began ending preferences for certain religions. Connecticut and New Hampshire ended state support of the Congregational Church in 1818 and 1819. Massachusetts did the same in 1833.[8] Meanwhile, membership in other churches grew.

Many links between church and state remained, though. Some states had religious tests. A person had to agree to certain beliefs to hold public jobs. Some tests continued into the mid-twentieth century. A Maryland law let people become notaries public only if they believed in God. It was not until

1961 that the Supreme Court declared that law unconstitutional.[9]

Other states would not let ministers hold public office. In 1978, the Supreme Court case of *McDaniel v. Paty* said that went against the Establishment Clause too. *McDaniel* held that a Tennessee law barring ministers from serving at a state constitutional convention was unconstitutional.[10]

Many immigrants came to America in the 1800s. First, many people came from Ireland and Germany. Later, many immigrants came from Italy and other countries in southern Europe. Many newcomers were Catholic.

The "Know-Nothing" party and other groups wanted to keep Catholics out. They disliked Catholics' loyalty to the pope, who heads their church. They feared the influx of people willing to work cheaply. That fear translated into prejudice against "foreigners."

Between 1830 and 1860, anti-Catholic feelings flared into violence. Mobs burned down two Catholic churches in Philadelphia. Protestants burned down a Catholic convent in Massachusetts. People also blew up churches in Dorchester, Massachusetts, and Sidney, Ohio.[11]

Public schools became part of American life in the 1800s. Most schools had a Protestant tone. Schools regularly taught lessons with Protestant versions of the Bible. Children prayed in school too.

In New York City, tax money went to public schools that taught Protestantism. Catholic parents wanted public funds for their own schools. The city's education board turned them down.[12] Nonetheless, the parents did not want the schools instilling Protestant beliefs in their children. As a result, Catholic schools grew in the city and elsewhere around the country.

Early Court Rulings

Few Supreme Court cases dealt with the First Amendment and religion in the 1800s. In 1878, the Court held that the federal government could limit Utah men to one wife. That went against Mormon beliefs, but the Court said it was all right. In its view, marriage was not just something religious, but also a civil contract upon which society is built. The government could not restrict people's religious beliefs, but it could limit their actions. Just as the government could forbid human sacrifices for religious purposes, so could it limit people to one marriage at a time. To apply the law differently based on each individual's belief would "permit every citizen to become a law unto himself."[13]

An 1892 case said a church could hire a minister from another country, even if the law otherwise forbade hiring foreigners. "This is a Christian nation," wrote Justice David Brewer, as he reviewed the country's religious background.[14]

Given that history, he could not believe that Congress meant to interfere with the right of any Catholic, Protestant, or Jewish group in bringing in religious leaders of their choice. That would unfairly burden religion.

An 1899 case let Roman Catholic nuns set up a hospital in Washington, D.C. That did not violate the Establishment Clause. Yes, the group was Catholic. But the hospital was a "purely secular one."[15] Tougher cases would come later.

A Shift in the Twentieth Century

America's ethnic and religious profile changed during the twentieth century. The number of denominations went from a few dozen to over a thousand.

Starting in 1940, the Supreme Court heard many cases on church and state. A 1947 case adopted Thomas Jefferson's language about a "wall of separation" between church and state. Later cases raised that wall high.

Groups feel differently about the Court's rulings. Some groups want strict separation of church and state. Others feel government should be more accommodating to religion. The next two chapters look at these views.

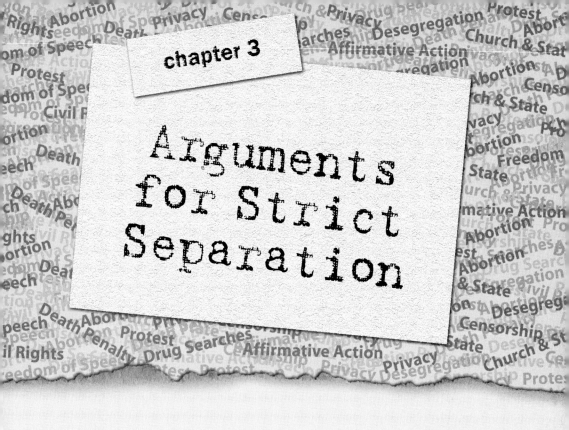

chapter 3

Arguments for Strict Separation

Strict separationists want a "wall" between church and state. What are their arguments?

Protecting People's Beliefs

Some people do not believe in God. They feel offended when the government appears to promote religion.

Many religious people want to keep church and state apart too. They believe that this protects their freedom.

"It's not hostile to religion to support the separation of church and state," stresses Steven Freeman. "It's a matter of valuing religion and everybody's right to have the religious views of their own choosing."[1] Freeman is the legal director for the Anti-Defamation League (ADL). The group started in 1913 to protect Jewish people. It fights many types of discrimination.

Many people may want public prayer. But the Constitution protects everyone. That includes groups that practice religions other than Christianity, which traditionally has had the most followers in the United States. It also includes people who may not practice any religion at all. "Freedom in practicing religion doesn't mean a lot if it only applies to the majority religion," says Jeremy Leaming at Americans United for Separation of Church and State.[2]

The Free Exercise Clause does a lot to protect freedom. But the Establishment Clause goes further. It protects people from having to pay any taxes to support religion. That way, people do not have to support beliefs they do not hold and may find repugnant.

According to separationists, government should not control religion. And religion should not rule the government. That way, all people can act according to their conscience.

No Coercion

"Governmentally established religions and religious persecutions go hand in hand," wrote Supreme Court Justice Hugo Black.[3] Persecution is rare in the United States now. But it has happened, even in recent years.

"It certainly happened in the aftermath of 9/11," says Freeman. "It happened to Muslim kids. It's happened to Jewish kids who've been victimized by anti-Semitism."[4]

Anti-Semitism is prejudice against Jewish people. And 9/11 refers to attacks by Arab terrorists in 2001. Hijacked jets crashed into the World Trade Center and the Pentagon. A fourth plane crashed in Pennsylvania.

Lisa Herdahl learned about persecution the hard way. She moved to Mississippi in 1993. She did not want her children taking part in Bible reading and daily prayers at the local public school.

People called the children "devil worshippers" and other names. Some friends stopped playing with them. Other children assaulted them. The family got bomb threats.

Herdahl sued in federal court. Judge Neal Biggers said the school prayers had to stop: "The Bill of Rights was created to protect the minority from tyranny by the majority."[5]

In 1998, an eleven-year-old girl complained that her public school teacher prayed and taught religion. The New York City school fired the teacher. But then other students harassed the girl.[6]

Even subtle pressure can make people in the minority feel uneasy. Technically, they may not be forced to take part in a religious exercise. But a school or other public setting may make them likely to "go along." They feel odd if they do not take part.

Separation of church and state is one way to avoid that pressure. Separationists feel it helps keep America free. In Justice John Paul Stevens's words:

> Whenever we remove a brick from the wall that was designed to separate religion and government, we increase the risk of religious strife and weaken the foundation of our democracy.[7]

Indeed, religious disputes played a part in many wars throughout history. Even in recent decades, religion played a role in conflicts in the Middle East, the former Yugoslavia, and Northern Ireland. Keeping church and state apart reduces the risk of strife, say separationists.

Protecting Diversity

"We're not like we were in 1787," says Jeremy Leaming at Americans United for Separation of Church and State.[8] Now the United States has many more religious groups. It is a very diverse country.

About 60 percent of Americans say they belong to an organized religion. Christian faiths make up about 90 percent of that number, with about 52 percent saying they are Protestant. Another 38 percent belong to the Roman Catholic Church.[9] Yet even among Christians, beliefs and tolerance for other sects vary widely.

Indeed, no one denomination is the largest religious group in every state. The Catholic Church might have the most followers in Rhode Island, while the Baptists lead in Virginia, and the Mormons make up the biggest church in Utah. But often, even a state's largest religious group has only a minority of the population.[10] And even if a group makes up a majority in some regions, it can still be a minority in some neighborhoods.

In short, the United States has no majority denomination. Some people are always in the minority somewhere. Separationists like Norman Redlich of the American Jewish Congress have argued that people should never feel like "religious strangers in their own home."[11] They feel that keeping church and state apart prevents that.

"Part of being in a pluralistic diverse society is respecting those who have different views," notes Freeman at the ADL.[12] If no group can promote its faith in a school or other public setting, everyone is on equal footing. That protects all Americans.

Good for Both Religion and Government

Roger Williams felt people could follow their conscience best when the government stayed out of religion. Philosopher John Locke from England felt that way too. "True and saving religion consists in the inward persuasion of the mind," he wrote.[13]

Basically, it would not be faith if government forced people to believe something.

"A union of government and religion tends to destroy government and to degrade religion," wrote Justice Black.[14] People with other beliefs grow to hate the government. And religions lose respect if they need the government's support to make people believe in them.

Beyond this, religious leaders do not want the government telling them what to do. If a state gives money to a group, for example, it can ask to see the group's accounting books. It may question a church group's actions.

Entanglement with the state could affect how churches act. A church may limit what it says on issues of social policy. It may make its actions more secular and less religious to get public funding. Arguably, that could weaken its mission.

At the same time, America has too many religions for all of them to get public benefits. After all, no government program has unlimited money. "So you are obviously putting the government in the position of picking and choosing," says Leaming. "And that can end up looking like favoritism at some point."[15]

Government does not want to get bogged down in religion either. Public officials have enough work to do. Separationists feel that dealing with church matters would be an added burden.

People elect their leaders to represent them. They do not want them to listen to any one church. Ideally, say separationists, leaders will listen to all people—whether they go to any church or not.

Supported by History

The First Amendment could have forbidden "a national religion." James Madison proposed that in one draft. But the language talks about "no law respecting an establishment of religion." This is closer to a proposal from Samuel Livermore of New Hampshire. He would have forbidden any laws "touching religion."[16]

Thomas Jefferson felt very strongly about keeping church and state apart. In 1802, he wrote to the Danbury Baptist Association:

> I contemplate with sovereign reverence that act of the whole American people which declared that their legislature should "make no law respecting an establishment of religion, or prohibiting the free exercise thereof," thus building a wall of separation between Church & State.[17]

Yes, history shows that the government did promote religion at times. Separationists say that does not make it right. The Constitution is the country's supreme law, and the First Amendment is part of that.

Separationists feel the First Amendment is clear. Church and state are separate under the Constitution. They should stay that way.

Prayer Is a Private Matter

Separation of church and state does not make America a godless society. Most Americans belong to a religion.[18] They just pray in different ways.

Students have always been able to pray in the public schools. A joke says they will keep praying as long as there are math tests. But students should pray on their own time, say separationists. They do not need the school's stamp of approval.

Some people see that as a limit. But students cannot do whatever they want at school anyway.

Separationists say that organized prayer does not belong in schools; the Supreme Court has agreed. This photograph of schoolchildren praying was taken in 1980 in Massachusetts.

Public schools and other government institutions must obey the Establishment Clause. That makes limits necessary, say separationists.

"There are certain instances where the government does have interests in regulating speech: when you try to incite violence; when you try to spur on illegal activity; child pornography," explains Leaming at Americans United for Separation of Church and State.[19] In his view, freedom of speech is not absolute. Separationists feel the government can and should limit speech to keep people from pushing prayer on others in public schools and other public forums.

Separationists stress their view that religion is a private matter. They feel it is best left to individuals and their families, not the government. "The easiest thing for public schools to do is to remain neutral in the matter," says Leaming.[20]

No Gray Areas

Separationists feel there are no gray areas under the Establishment Clause. Like Thomas Jefferson, they want a "wall of separation" between church and state. They do not stop at saying there can be no official church. Like Justice Black, they feel government cannot "pass laws which aid one religion, aid all religions, or prefer one religion over another."[21]

By this view, even nondenominational prayers

go against the First Amendment. (Those are "generic" prayers that are not specific to any religious group.) These prayers try to find common ground among different faiths. Yet the prayers still offend people who do not believe in God.

Some religious people may take offense too. If someone's faith calls for saying certain prayers, why should that person say a generic prayer? Drinking watered-down milk does not give the body adequate nourishment. Saying watered-down prayers may not satisfy someone's soul, they say.

In short, separationists feel the government cannot give even a little nod to religion. A little nod could lead to a bigger stamp of approval. In the end, that could hurt everyone's freedom.

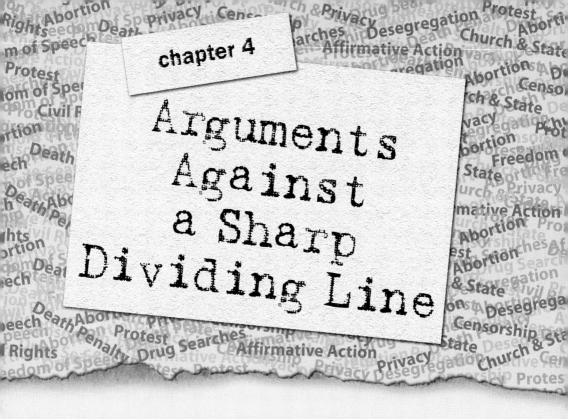

chapter 4

Arguments Against a Sharp Dividing Line

Most Americans feel the United States should not have an official church. Most of them would not want to see any religious group persecuted in America either. But some groups feel that separation of church and state can go too far. They would prefer that the government make some reasonable allowances for religion. Or, in other words, they would like government to be more accommodating to religion. Thus, people who oppose a sharp dividing line between church and state are sometimes called "accommodationists."

Protecting the Free Exercise of Religion

The First Amendment says there will be no establishment of religion. In the next phrase it guarantees the free exercise of religion. Accommodationists feel that a sharp dividing line between church and state can bring these two rights into conflict.

"Separation of church and state is a good thing," notes John Whitehead, president of The Rutherford Institute, a group that provides legal representation in various cases on church and state. "But the Establishment Clause should not be used as a bludgeon essentially to wipe out free exercise in the schools or any public places."[1]

Being told to pray in private is not enough, some people say. They believe that free exercise includes the right to pray in public.

"If a student can't pray out loud, then their faith is meaningless," says Whitehead.[2] Indeed, he feels, such rules send the message that prayer is inferior to other activities. No one should make any person feel that a desire to pray in school or any other public setting is wrong. People should never have to feel ashamed to pray.

In short, government should not make people pray. But it should not tell them when, where, and how to pray either, say accommodationists. Our democracy has no place for any prayer police.

Protecting Free Speech

The First Amendment also guarantees freedom of speech. When people pray in public, that is a kind of speech.

"We believe that the free speech clause and the free exercise clause are really combined now," says Whitehead at The Rutherford Institute. "If you allow expressive activities that are secular, you have to allow expressive activities by students that are religious."[3]

Such reasoning is behind the Equal Access Act. Congress passed the law in 1984. Basically, it lets student groups with a religious message use school facilities on the same terms as other groups. The Supreme Court upheld the law in 1990.[4]

Yes, the right to free speech has limits. But those limits apply to harmful types of speeches. Speech to incite violence is not protected. Neither is obscenity.

But prayer does not fall into that category, say accommodationists. People who pray feel it is sacred. No one in government has the right to treat prayer as if it were harmful or dangerous, they say.

Yes, religious speech can make other people feel like outsiders. It can make them feel uncomfortable. But accommodationists feel the government should not limit how and when people can pray or speak about their faith. People can state their political ideas in public forums, even if other people disagree with them. And in public schools, teachers assign literature or other reading with ideas some students may find disturbing. Why should

that states could not have laws respecting an establishment of religion. (The Supreme Court had not yet said that the Establishment Clause covered states too.) Justice Clarence Thomas has argued that anti-Catholic feelings lay behind the proposed Blaine Amendment.[12]

Not until 1947 did a Supreme Court case finally use Jefferson's words about a "wall of separation" between church and state. Justice Hugo Black wrote the majority opinion in that case.[13] Critics like Philip Hamburger at the University of Chicago have questioned his motives.[14] Black once belonged to the Ku Klux Klan. Among other things, the KKK held racist, anti-Catholic, and anti-Semitic views.

Does this mean that Justice Black was prejudiced against Catholics? Some of his comments suggest at least that he felt very wary. Consider his dissent in a case allowing public money to pay for textbooks in parochial schools, many of which were Catholic. Among other things, he railed against "powerful sectarian religious propagandists . . . looking toward complete domination and supremacy of their particular brand of religion."[15] Accommodationists question whether his strict stance on separation was truly neutral.

In short, the First Amendment has stayed the same for over two hundred years. But its application has changed over time. Accommodationists say history never required a wall of separation. To the contrary, they feel a wall is neither practical nor desirable.

Civil Religion

References to God are part of American life. Patriotic songs thank God for blessing America. Legislatures and courts include references to God in proceedings. Even the Supreme Court starts each session with a plea: "God save the United States and this Honorable Court."[16]

In large part, these are rituals. They are part of the pomp and ceremony that go with running a government. They command respect. They make public events more solemn.

Philosopher Jean-Jacques Rousseau called this kind of thing "civil religion."[17] Derek Davis at Baylor University feels it can be a good thing.

"We think of God as sovereign over all things— not just people, but over institutions too, including government," says Davis. "So we have this built-in need to see our government working in tandem with divine principles."

Otherwise, people would not trust the government. "In other words, if we see it out of step with heaven, we lose confidence in it," says Davis.[18] Aside from this, though, Davis wants separation of church and state.

People who do not believe in God object to such

references. One could argue that any harm is minimal. Or one could say that such references are not really prayer. On the other hand, many people take great pride in these traditions. They would feel hurt if they disappeared from public life.

In Need of a Moral Compass

Without religion in schools and public life, has America lost its moral compass? The United States has many problems, including drugs, crime, and failing schools. Has secularism—the exclusion of religion—made these problems worse?

Protestant minister Billy Graham raised this fear in the 1960s. Two Supreme Court cases had

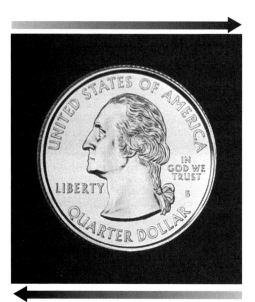

ruled against prayer in public schools. "The trend of taking God and moral teaching from the schools is a diabolical scheme," Graham said in 1963, "and it is bearing its fruit in the deluge of juvenile delinquency which is over-whelming our nation."[19]

While Graham's criticism softened in later years, some people still feel that way. Families do not always teach values at home. Schools sometimes

Accommodationists point out that religion is part of American public life. Even our money has the motto, "In God we trust."

try to fill the gap. Can schools really teach values without religion?

Of course, many people feel they can lead moral lives even if they do not belong to an organized religion. But religious values are at the heart of many laws. They affect policies on marriage, child welfare, crime, and other issues. If church and state were totally separate, would laws be just?

More recently, Judge Diarmuid O'Scannlain of the Ninth Circuit Court of Appeals worried that forbidding references to God in schools could create "a distorted impression about the place of religion in our national life." He felt that would give atheism "a favored status" and create "a bias *against* religion." "One wonders then," he wrote, "does atheism become the default religion protected by the Establishment Clause?"[20]

This concern may not win many points in court. Yet it is a fear that many people feel strongly.

Accommodation Is Acceptable

Help for a religious group is not an automatic violation of the Constitution. A benefit can pass constitutional scrutiny if a law or practice is neutral on its face.

The 1947 case of *Everson* v. *Board of Education of Ewing Township* spoke about a wall of separation between church and state.[21] But even that case let public school districts bus children to religious schools. That helped the religious schools indirectly. But the children got the direct benefit. Basically, the law was neutral on religion.

In a related vein, government can indirectly help religious groups where the goal is not to promote religion, but some other valid purpose. Religious groups do a lot of good educational, social, and other work. Their efforts help society. They complement government activity. Thus, courts do not rule against all programs that have some benefit to religion. Rather, they look at the law's secular purpose.

If government should be neutral, some groups say, then it should accept churches as they are. It should not impose strict government standards. Churches should not have to change their mission or who they are.[22] This argument would give faith-based charities more government money with fewer strings attached.

But drawing lines can get tricky. When does accommodation stop and establishment begin?

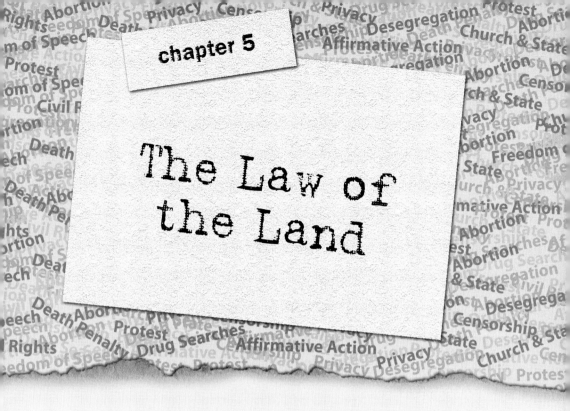

chapter 5

The Law of the Land

The Constitution is the supreme law of the land. It limits what the federal government can do. It limits the states and local governments too.

No law can conflict with the Constitution. Otherwise, that law is unconstitutional. An unconstitutional law is invalid. No one can enforce it.

No Single Test

The Supreme Court has the final say on what the Constitution means. The First Amendment deals with religion and free speech. It deals with freedom of association and the press too.

The First Amendment says Congress cannot make any law "respecting an establishment of religion." Congress cannot prohibit the free exercise of

49

religion either. Courts say this includes the whole federal government.

This goes for the states too. This is because the Fourteenth Amendment makes most of the Bill of Rights binding on the states. The Supreme Court made this clear in a 1940 case about passing out religious literature.[1]

The Supreme Court has no single test for Establishment Clause cases. Many cases use a three-part test from the 1971 case, *Lemon* v. *Kurtzman*.[2] *Lemon* overturned state programs to pay some costs for teaching nonreligious subjects in private schools. The Court said judges should ask three questions:

◇ Does a law have a secular purpose?

◇ Does the primary effect neither advance nor inhibit religion?

◇ Does it avoid excessive entanglement between church and state?

If the answer to all three questions is yes, the *Lemon* test says a law can stand under the Establishment Clause.

Various cases use the *Lemon* test. Yet some cases give less weight to the third part on entanglement. Otherwise, steps to make sure public money did not support religion could be seen as too much government involvement. In other words, checking to make sure the program followed the First Amendment could arguably be grounds to condemn it. That would be a "Catch-22," or a no-win situation.[3]

Neutrality is another test. The government cannot endorse religious beliefs. It cannot act hostile to them either. The test allows incidental benefits to churches, as long as the law is neutral.

The Supreme Court has used these ideas to let private groups express religious beliefs on public property. It wants to protect the right to free speech, including religious speech. If the government is just letting private groups or individuals have their say, that does not violate the Constitution.[4]

The neutrality test also lets public money go to some religious welfare organizations. If they meet all the same standards as other groups, their religious ties do not disqualify them. Colleges sometimes benefit with this test too, when individual students choose where to use grants or loans.

Another test could be to ask if the government is preferring one religion over another. But Supreme Court cases have said the government cannot promote religion in general either.[5] Plus, people who believe in no religion could argue that the government was discriminating against their lack of faith.

Another view would ask if there was any coercion. Yet this test does not solve the problem, because people disagree about what is coercive. Some people might say coercion is forcing someone to do something. Others might interpret any official action as a type of coercion.

Exemptions From the Law

As a practical matter, America has never had a solid wall between church and state. Various laws limit what churches and their members can do. Other laws help religious groups by promoting the free exercise of religion or free speech.

Still other laws try to maintain a balance. They try not to promote religion. But they also aim to avoid extra burdens on it.

Tax exemptions are a case in point. Most churches in the United States are set up as non-profit organizations. Section 501(c)(3) of the Internal Revenue Code says that qualifying groups do not have to pay federal taxes. The law helps churches financially.

The exemption has a broader goal. Churches often have socially worthwhile programs. The tax exemption also covers other groups that help society. Charitable, educational, and scientific purposes qualify too.

The tax exemption has strings attached. It limits political activities. Churches cannot endorse candidates in elections. They cannot unlawfully discriminate based on race, either.[6]

Most states and local governments also give a property tax exemption to churches. The

Supreme Court has said that such exemptions are constitutional. In effect, they make it easier for churches to exist. That promotes the free exercise of religion. In *Walz* v. *Tax Commission*, the Court wrote:

> The grant of a tax exemption is not sponsorship since the government does not transfer part of its revenue to churches but simply abstains from demanding that the church support the state.[7]

The laws avoid entanglement too. States and local governments do not have to think about what to do with churches' property if they do not pay their taxes. States cannot squash churches through high taxes either.

Military draft laws said people did not have to serve if it went against their consciences. At first the law looked at what religions taught. But Supreme Court cases said to look at people's sincere beliefs instead. That way, the exemption would not favor some religions over others.[8]

Amish people do not believe in sending children to school after eighth grade. In 1972, the Supreme Court held that a state could not make the children go anyway.[9] That exception to the rule was not an establishment of religion. Rather, it protected the Amish people's free exercise of religion.

Amish people also believe they have a duty to care for their old and needy people. The law said self-employed Amish people did not have to pay

Social Security taxes. However, in 1982, the Supreme Court said the exemption did not apply when an Amish person employed other people, even if they were Amish too.[10] The government had a compelling interest in making sure people paid into the system.

Other cases overturn accommodations for a single group. Most children in the village of Kiryas Joel went to Hasidic Jewish schools. Handicapped children could get special help. But they would have to go to public schools outside the village. That made them uncomfortable.

To help, a New York law made the village its own school district. The special education teachers could help students inside the village. In 1994, the Supreme Court said the law was unconstitutional.[11] It was not neutral. It advanced religion for a single group.

A later Supreme Court case let special education teachers help children on-site at religious schools.[12] As a practical matter, that 1997 case eased the tension.

Limits on Activities

Some laws can limit church activities. In principle, most people want as few restrictions as possible. The fewer the restrictions, they feel, the more free people are to practice their faith.

In 1993, the Supreme Court voided a Florida

city law against all animal sacrifice. The city had valid health and safety interests. But its law went too far. Basically, it tried to outlaw Santeria, a religion that combines Roman Catholic ceremonies with elements of African spiritualism. "The First Amendment forbids an official purpose to disapprove of a particular religion or of religion in general," wrote Justice Anthony Kennedy.[13]

Zoning cases are less sensational. But they also show how churches must obey various laws. In 1997, the Supreme Court held that a Texas church had to obey historical landmark restrictions. A law that tried to exempt churches from the limits was invalid.[14]

When laws do apply to churches, they should be enforced equally. The government cannot play favorites. It cannot treat some churches better than others. For example, a Minnesota law said churches would have to register under a state statute unless they got at least half their money from members or related organizations. The state wanted to police private groups' fund-raising practices. But in *Larson* v. *Valente*, the Supreme Court said the Establishment Clause forbid such distinctions among religions.[15] The state could not prefer some religious denominations over others.

In *Fowler* v. *Rhode Island*, the Supreme Court struck down a Pawtucket law that the city used to keep a Jehovah's Witness from preaching in a park. After all, the city would let other religious groups meet and pray in the park if they wanted. In the Court's view,

> To call the words which one minister speaks to his congregation a sermon, immune from regulation, and the words of another minister an address, subject to regulation, is merely an indirect way of preferring one religion over another.[16]

Churches cannot tell the government what to do, either. A Massachusetts law said that businesses would not get liquor licenses if a church located within 500 feet objected. The law was an

These Amish children are walking home after going shopping. The Supreme Court ruled in 1972 that a state could not make Amish children attend school after the eighth grade.

effort to avoid disputes with churches that did not want bars nearby. In 1982, the Supreme Court said churches could not have that veto power.[17]

Internal Affairs

The government cannot run religions. Thus, courts shy away from getting tied up in internal church matters.

The case of *Watson* v. *Jones* arose just after the Civil War. The dispute was about who owned the property of a Presbyterian church in Louisville, Kentucky. The case would have required deciding whose interpretation of the church's laws was correct. In 1871, the Supreme Court said the courts should not take sides on matters of theology: "The law knows no heresy, and is committed to the support of no dogma, the establishment of no sect."[18] The church's internal ruling stood.

Later cases reached similar results. A 1952 case set aside a law that affected the U.S. head of the Russian Orthodox Church.[19] A 1976 case said an Illinois court could not prevent a bishop's dismissal.[20]

Courts do not always have to keep "hands off." In 1979, *Jones* v. *Wolf* said courts can decide property questions with "neutral principles of law."[21] If a matter touches on doctrine or church leadership, though, courts should avoid the fray.

The Civil Rights Act of 1964 says employers

cannot discriminate on the grounds of religion. But churches have an exception. They can hire persons whose religious views they prefer. In 1987, the Supreme Court upheld that exception under the Establishment Clause.[22] It promotes the free exercise of religion. Plus, it reduces government involvement in churches' internal affairs.

Church leaders are not above the law, however. Headlines in 2002 and 2003 exposed cases where Catholic priests were accused of—and in some cases convicted of—abusing children.[23] In some cases, church officials kept claims quiet. Catholic dioceses said they wanted to discipline priests under their own rules, but states could still press criminal charges when they learned about the assaults. Victims' families sued various priests. In some cases, they sued other church leaders and dioceses too, claiming there was a duty to report abuse and remove offenders from service.[24]

Federal, state, and local laws raise many other issues about church and state. The next chapter looks at cases about schools. Chapter 7 looks at religion in the public square. The Constitution controls all those cases.

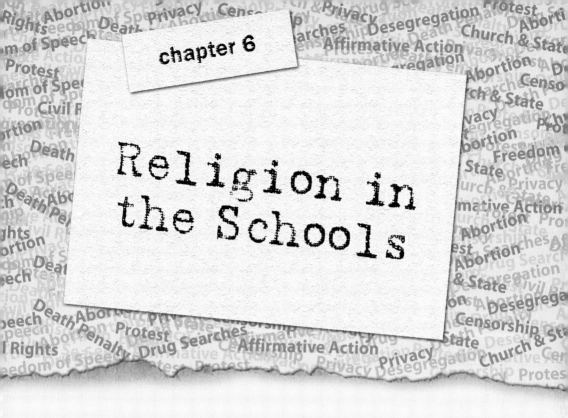

chapter 6

Religion in the Schools

Most people do not want public schools to teach any specific religion. Can students still pray? And what about private religious schools—can states help their students?

Prayer Wars

Many public schools used to have daily prayer. Often they had Bible reading too. That began to change in 1948.

In *Illinois* ex rel. *McCollum* v. *Board of Education*, the Court said church groups could not teach religion during public school class time. Illinois schools let religious groups teach during class time in tax-supported buildings. They gave the church groups a ready-made audience of students.

"This is not separation of Church and State," wrote Justice Hugo Black.[1]

In 1952, *Zorach* v. *Clauson* upheld the practice of "released time"—letting students leave their regular classes to receive religious instruction.[2] The main difference between *McCollum* and *Zorach* was where the religious teaching took place. But the Supreme Court felt that forbidding released time would be hostile to religion.

Even if they did not teach religion, many public schools wanted children to pray. *Engel* v. *Vitale* dealt with a prayer written by the New York Board of Regents. It said:

> Almighty God, we acknowledge our dependence upon Thee, and we beg Thy blessings upon us, our parents, our teachers and our Country.[3]

The Board of Regents felt this general prayer would not offend people. Although classes had to say the prayer if their school district directed, no child had to say the prayer. They could stay silent or leave the room. Nonetheless, five families sued. In 1962, the Supreme Court ruled that the prayer was unconstitutional.[4]

The Court's opinion in *Engel* v. *Vitale* noted that the prayer did not help any one religion. But the schools could not promote religion in general either.

The next year, the Court looked at a Pennsylvania law on Bible reading in schools. The same case looked at a Baltimore, Maryland, law. It said that students in schools should say the Lord's Prayer each day.

Abington School District v. *Schempp* struck down both laws. The states' job was to "maintain strict neutrality, neither aiding nor opposing religion."[5] They could not hold religious exercises.

Justice Potter Stewart dissented. He worried about a "religion of secularism." Should schools teach that only worldly things are important? And why should the Court side with those people who felt others should pray only in private?[6]

Many people approved of *Engel* and *Schempp*. Many church leaders were in that camp. Other people felt outraged. While many Protestant ministers supported the rulings, others, like Billy Graham, said the holding was "wrong." Catholic Cardinal Francis Spellman worried that the case "will do great harm to our country." New York Representative Frank Becker even introduced a constitutional amendment on prayer.[7]

Public schools could not make students say any particular prayer. Could they allow time "for meditation or voluntary prayer"? The Supreme Court struck down such a law in *Wallace* v. *Jaffree*. The law had no secular purpose, wrote Justice John Paul Stevens in 1985. Reviewing the legislative history, he found that the law's goal was "to return prayer to the public schools."[8] In other words, the law failed the *Lemon* test. It did not have a secular purpose, and its primary purpose was to promote religion.

Chief Justice Warren Burger and several other justices disagreed. "Without pressuring those who do not wish to pray, the statute simply creates an opportunity to think, to plan, or to pray if one wishes," wrote Burger, "as Congress does by providing chaplains and chapels."[9]

Over twelve years later, some states still had moment-of-silence laws. A Georgia law allowed a "moment of silent reflection" in public schools. But the law expressly said that was not meant as a religious service. A 1997 appeals court case upheld the law.[10] In short, a daily moment of silence can be all right, as long as there is no obvious intent to promote prayer.

Lee v. *Weisman* looked at graduation ceremonies. When Deborah Weisman graduated from middle school, the principal invited a Jewish rabbi to pray. Deborah's family was Jewish, but her father still objected. He filed suit.

In 1992, the Supreme Court held that graduation prayers went against the First Amendment. It does not matter if most people want prayer. Just having to stay silent while someone prays could make a student feel forced into taking part. Justice Anthony Kennedy wrote:

> What to most believers may seem nothing more than a reasonable request that the nonbeliever respect

their religious practices, in a school context may appear to the nonbeliever or dissenter to be an attempt to employ the machinery of the State to enforce a religious orthodoxy.[11]

Could students themselves pray at events like football games? *Santa Fe Independent School District v. Doe* tackled this question in 2000. A Texas high school let elected students say prayers at football games and graduations. The Supreme Court said that was unconstitutional.

The practice of letting students vote on who would pray put the minority "at the mercy of the majority," wrote Justice Stevens. Beyond this, the practice gave the school's stamp of approval to the prayers. "In actuality, it constitutes prayer sponsored by the school."[12]

Equal Access

Public schools cannot sponsor prayer. Do they have to give students a place to pray? Some cases say yes.

Prayer is not just the exercise of religion. It is also a form of speech. In 1984, Congress passed the Equal Access Act.[13] It applied to all public high schools that got federal funds and let various student groups meet. Those schools could not ban student groups based on the religious, political, or other content of their speech.

An Omaha, Nebraska, high school let about thirty groups meet on school grounds. Each group needed a faculty advisor. Bridget Mergens wanted to form a Christian club, but without a faculty advisor. That way, the school would not be promoting religion. The school said no.

In 1990, the Supreme Court ruled for the students. The school would not support religion by letting the club meet. Rather, it would promote the students' free exercise and free speech rights. Justice Sandra Day O'Connor wrote:

> There is a crucial difference between government speech endorsing religion, which the Establishment Clause forbids, and private speech endorsing religion, which the Free Speech and Free Exercise Clauses protect. We think that secondary school students are mature enough and are likely to understand that a school does not endorse or support student speech that it merely permits on a nondiscriminatory basis.[14]

The Equal Access Act was constitutional, held the Court.

Lamb's Chapel v. *Center Moriches Union Free School District* went a step further. A Long Island school district let community groups meet on its property outside of school hours. It kept religious groups out.

A Christian church wanted to show films on family issues at the school. In 1993, the Supreme Court ruled in favor of the church. The school could not keep the films out because of their religious viewpoint.[15]

Rosenberger v. *Rector and Visitors of the University of Virginia* dealt with a similar issue at the college level.[16] All students paid an activity fee. Ronald Rosenberger wanted money from the fund for a Christian journal called *Wide Awake*. The school said no.

In 1995, the Supreme Court sided with Rosenberger. The school could not discriminate based on his viewpoint. Giving his group money was not an establishment of religion. The dissent felt the state should not pay to publish anything that preached religion.

In general, the Supreme Court has worried less about the Establishment Clause in cases about college students. Most of them are legally adults. They seem less vulnerable to subtle pressure. Plus, many college courses seem separate from religion, even at religious colleges. Thus, a 1981 case said public universities could not keep out student religious clubs if they let other clubs use the facilities.[17]

Do arguments about discrimination against religious viewpoints carry the same force when younger students are involved? Consider a 2001 case, *Good News Club* v. *Milford Central School*. A school policy let groups use the building after hours. The Good News Club was a Christian club for children aged six to twelve. They wanted to meet in the cafeteria once a week. They would sing songs, hear a Bible lesson, and learn scripture.

The school district said no. The meetings would be a form of worship. The Supreme Court said that violated the right to free speech.

The school was a limited public forum. "Limited" meant it did not have to let everyone in. But the school's restrictions had to be reasonable. The school could not pick and choose among viewpoints.

Teaching morals and values was within the school's guidelines. For example, the school would have let a club discuss Aesop's fables. Scout groups could meet too. The school said no to the Good News Club just because it was religious. This was "impermissible viewpoint discrimination."[18]

Separation of church and state was no excuse to keep the club out, said the Supreme Court. The club was not a school activity. Children would not feel forced to attend. Indeed, they needed their parents' permission to go. Thus, *Good News Club* protects students' free speech and the free exercise of religion.

The number of students involved in *Good News Club* was limited. But what if almost all students stayed after school for a religious club? Could the club become an "unofficial" last period for teaching religion? Would that pressure any children who did not go? How different would that case be from the 1948 *McCollum* case that ruled against teaching religion in public schools?[19]

Science or Religion?

Where did we come from? How was the world created? Science classes raise these questions. But they are touchy topics with some groups.

Some religious groups believe people should interpret the Bible literally. If Genesis says God created the world in seven days, they take it at face value. They do not see "seven days" as a metaphor or artful phrase. They deny the theory of evolution.

In contrast, most scientists accept the theory of evolution. Simply stated, the theory is that life-forms developed over millions of years from common ancestors. Life-forms that adapted well to their environments lived long enough to reproduce.

Charles Darwin presented the theory in 1859 in his book *On the Origin of Species*. Scientists have since found lots of evidence to support the theory. They have developed it further too. For example, chance plays a big role in how species adapt and evolve.

Evolution is a theory, in that no one can go back in time to prove exactly how things happened. But it is also science. Evidence and facts support it. No scientific evidence contradicts the theory of evolution.

In 1925, a Tennessee court decided *Scopes* v.

State, the famous "monkey trial" case.[20] The state's highest court reversed a teacher's conviction on technical grounds. Yet it held that the state could forbid the teaching of evolution.

Scientific evidence for evolution mounted. In 1957, the Soviet Union launched *Sputnik* and the space age began. States updated their science curricula. Many states now taught evolution. Yet some states resisted.

In the 1960s, Susan Epperson wanted to teach a chapter on evolution to her tenth-grade biology class. A 1928 Arkansas law said that would be a crime. In *Epperson* v. *Arkansas*, the Supreme Court sided with Epperson. Teaching could not be "tailored" to any religious group or belief. The statute was unconstitutional.[21]

Edwards v. *Aguillard* went further.[22] In 1987, the Supreme Court said a Louisiana law could not make schools give "balanced treatment" to both evolution and "creation science." The law's purpose was to promote religion. It could not stand.

"Disclaimer" laws have met challenges too. Under those laws, teachers would have to say evolution is a theory. They would have to announce that children can still believe what their religion teaches. At least one federal court has said such laws violate the First Amendment.[23]

Groups in some states want schools to teach "intelligent design." The concept does not directly discuss God. It says that some intelligent design caused Earth's many complex life-forms.[24] Schools that teach the concept would likely face court challenges.

Social studies classes also raise questions. Children need to learn about different cultures. Often that touches on religion.

In one case, parents sued over stories and activities about Hindu gods and Buddha. They complained that Earth Day programs promoted worship of the Earth as if it were a god. They also objected when pupils made worry dolls, or charms. A federal appeals court said the high school's Earth Day program was secular, not religious. It did not rule on other complaints because the families had since moved out of the district.[25]

Controversies will continue to come up. In general, public schools can teach about different cultures. Teachers can talk about religious traditions. But they cannot endorse them. Otherwise, that would cross the line separating church and state.

Private School Students

About 10 percent of American students go to private grade schools.[26] Religious groups run many of those schools. They can teach what they want about religion.

How far can states go to help students at religious schools? The Supreme Court has said tax money can pay for nonreligious books for the students. This aid allows schools to charge lower tuition, but the Court felt that is just an indirect benefit. The direct beneficiaries are children and their parents.[27]

Likewise, children benefit from bus rides to religious schools. *Everson* v. *Board of Education* allowed that, even as it said there must be a "wall of separation" between church and state.[28]

In 1971, *Lemon* v. *Kurtzman* said states could not directly help religious schools, even in secular subjects.[29] They cannot give religious schools money to boost salaries for teachers of math, foreign languages, science, or gym.

Chief Justice Warren Burger's opinion set forth the three-prong *Lemon* test: Is a law's purpose secular? Is its primary effect to promote or inhibit religion? Is there excessive entanglement of church and state?

In *Lemon*, the aid program had too much risk for fostering religion. The Court wrote:

> Under our system the choice has been made that government is to be entirely excluded from the area of religious instruction and churches excluded from the affairs of government. The Constitution decrees that religion must be a private matter for the individual, the family, and the institutions of private choice, and that while some involvement and entanglement are inevitable, lines must be drawn.[30]

The same day that the Supreme Court issued its opinion in the *Lemon* case, *Tilton* v. *Richardson* upheld a federal program that gave construction grants to colleges. Private religious colleges could qualify if buildings and facilities would be used for secular purposes.

Chief Justice Warren Burger noted:

> There are generally significant differences between the religious aspects of church-related institutions of higher learning and parochial elementary and secondary schools. College students are less impressionable and less susceptible to religious indoctrination.[31]

He also stressed the nature of college and post-graduate courses, plus the atmosphere of many colleges' academic freedom. Thus, the Court made a distinction between younger and older students.

After *Lemon*, the Court held that other forms of aid for parochial school students were unconstitutional too. A 1973 case held states could not give tax credits to families for private-school tuition.[32] A 1977 case said tax money could not pay for private-school field trips.[33]

In later years, courts have allowed a broader range of help. For example, a 1983 case upheld a Minnesota program that gave tax deductions for parents paying children's school expenses. Parents could get the deduction if their children went to public or private schools, even if the private schools were religious. Families with public school children would likely have lower expenses than those whose children attended private schools. Yet *Mueller* v. *Allen* let the program stand.[34]

States can give also special educational services to private school students. This can include speech therapy, remedial reading help, psychological services, or other aid. For example, *Zobrest* v. *Catalina Foothills School District* upheld paying a sign language interpreter with public funds to help a teen at a religious school.[35]

A 1997 case let New York City send public school teachers into religious schools to give remedial help. An earlier case had said there would be "excessive entanglement" if teachers went into the private schools. *Agostini* v. *Felton* held that was no longer good law.[36] In the *Agostini* program, supervisors made sure the publicly paid teachers did not teach any religion.

In 2000, *Mitchell* v. *Helms* held that religious schools could use computers, library materials, and other equipment bought with public money.[37] The same equipment could be used in public schools. Thus, the Court found, there was no problem letting private religious schools have it too.

Dissenting opinions talked about the pervasively religious nature of the schools. In other words, they felt that the religious nature of a school necessarily affects everything that goes on there. What would stop schools from using some items for religious purposes too? But those arguments were in the minority.

In 2002, the Court went even further. In *Zelman v. Simmons-Harris*, it approved a voucher plan that let certain Ohio students attend private schools instead of their own failing public schools.[38] Chapter 8 looks at the case in detail.

Meanwhile, the Court has continued to approve aid programs that indirectly help private religious colleges. Cases after *Tilton v. Richardson* let

In Lemon v. Kurtzman, *the Court ruled against a state program for aid to religious schools. However, later rulings said that religious schools could use equipment bought with public money. These students attend a parochial school in Maine.*

religious colleges get grants or benefit from tax-free bonds as long as facilities were not for religious purposes.[39]

Often students getting financial aid through federal or state programs can use it at religious universities too. In 1986, *Witters v. Washington Department of Services for the Blind* held that the state of Washington would not violate the Establishment Clause by paying for vocational rehabilitation services when a student went to a religious college.[40] In 2004, the Supreme Court confirmed that states can have a scholarship program that lets students use funds at either religious or secular schools. However, said *Locke v. Davey*, a state may limit its program and deny aid to students majoring in theology.[41]

In short, the government can give some help for private school students. But plans must be neutral. Also, the Court has split on various issues. And the Court's makeup can change. Debates about church and state in the schools will go on.

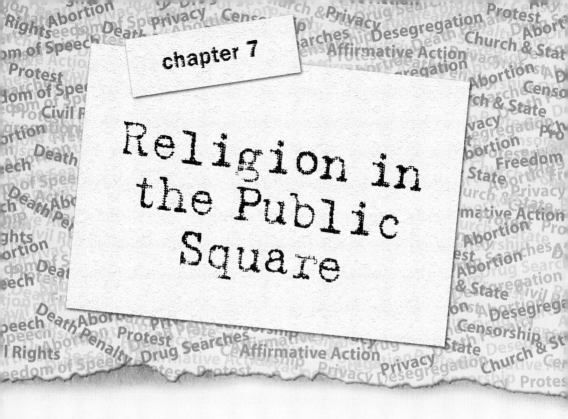

chapter 7

Religion in the Public Square

Questions about church and state go beyond the school setting. Can government forums show religious symbols? When is prayer allowed?

Showdown Over the Ten Commandments

Judge Roy Moore posted the Ten Commandments in his courtroom in Etowah County, Alabama. Christian and Jewish people believe that God gave those laws to Moses long ago. Moore felt that the rules form the basis for modern law. Two lawsuits challenged Moore's action. Moore won.

Later, Moore ran as the "Ten Commandments Judge" for chief justice of the Alabama Supreme Court. Soon after winning, Moore put a huge monument with the commandments in the rotunda of the State Judicial Building. The monument was about three feet wide, three feet deep, and four feet tall. It weighed over two and a half tons.

In Moore's view, public officials have a right to state their religious views. They just could not force those views on other people. Besides, the state did not pay for the statue.

Three lawyers sued in federal court. They felt offended by the monument. It made them feel like outsiders. They won their challenge. The trial court ruled that the monument went against the Establishment Clause, and the court of appeals agreed. The Ten Commandments are a sacred text. The judge could not display them like that.[1]

The court relied on a 1980 Supreme Court case, *Stone* v. *Graham.* That case held that a Kentucky law about posting the Ten Commandments in public schools was void. Fine print under each display said the rules had "secular" meaning. That did not save the law. "The preeminent purpose for posting the Ten Commandments on schoolroom walls is plainly religious in nature," the Court found.[2]

Judge Moore refused to remove the monument. Other court officials took it away. Judge Moore then faced disciplinary charges. Alabama's judicial panel voted unanimously to remove him from office. A sitting judge could not flaunt a federal court order. That would undermine the law.

Interestingly, the Ten Commandments show up in other public places, including the Supreme Court. But other symbols surround it. The religious detail is not the main focus.

The Supreme Court will continue to review cases on this issue.[3] The Court's rulings will guide future cases.

The Reindeer Rule

End-of-the-year holidays are a time for parties and good cheer. But when it comes to holiday displays, people on both sides of the church-state debate can seem like grinches.

Each year, a holiday display in Pawtucket, Rhode Island, welcomed downtown shoppers with the message, "SEASONS GREETINGS." For at least forty years, a nativity scene had been part of the display. It showed baby Jesus, Mary, and Joseph. It had shepherds, angels, wise men, and animals too.

The city owned the nativity set. The display was in a privately owned park. Some city residents and the American Civil Liberties Union sued.

In 1984, *Lynch* v. *Donnelly* held that the display did not go against the First Amendment. After all, Christmas was a national holiday. And the display was not all religious. It had reindeer pulling Santa's sleigh. It had candy-cane poles. It had a

Christmas tree. Overall, the display attracted shoppers. It boosted business.

"The display is sponsored by the city to celebrate the Holiday and to depict the origins of that Holiday," wrote Chief Justice Burger. "These are legitimate secular purposes."[4]

Four of the nine justices disagreed. The nativity set was a religious symbol. That did not change just because plastic reindeer and other secular symbols surrounded it.

Also, the display could offend many people. Non-Christians do not believe that Jesus is God. Yet even devout Christians could find the display "insulting." To them, reindeer, Santa, and other secular symbols take away from the sacred meaning of Christmas.[5]

In 1989, the Supreme Court said a stand-alone nativity went against the First Amendment. It had prominent place in a county courthouse. That showed improper government approval.

Meanwhile, other symbols sat outside a building owned jointly by the county and the city of Pittsburgh. They included a Christmas tree and a menorah. That did not violate the Establishment Clause.[6]

Several years later, the Ku Klux Klan wanted to display a cross on Capitol Square in Columbus during December. The state of Ohio said no. Yet it had already said other groups could put up a Christmas tree and a menorah.

In 1995, the Supreme Court said the state could not turn down the cross. While the Klan's political views may have driven the state's decision, the Court focused only on the Establishment Clause question. Capitol Square was a limited public forum. And the cross display would be "purely *private* religious speech."[7]

In sum, public holiday displays can show religious symbols with nonreligious ones. But drawing the line on what the Establishment Clause allows can be hard. If government allows religious symbols in a holiday display, some groups can feel left out. If it forbids private groups from making religious references, then they might object, too, because the government will not allow all views.[8]

Government-Sponsored Prayer

Since 1789, chaplains have led the House and Senate in prayer. Congress also has chapels for its members. All this has been at taxpayer expense.

If Congress can do this, shouldn't states be able to do it too? The United States Supreme Court said yes in 1983.

In *Marsh* v. *Chambers*, the Court said the Nebraska legislature could start each workday by having a government-paid chaplain say a prayer. Chief Justice Burger noted that the first federal law for paid chaplains passed three days before Congress agreed on the language for the Bill of Rights. He stated,

> Clearly the men who wrote the First Amendment Religion Clauses did not view paid legislative chaplains and opening prayers as a violation of that Amendment, for the practice of opening sessions with prayer has continued without interruption ever since that early session of Congress.[9]

Chief Justice Berger also cited an 1853 Senate Judiciary Committee report, which took the view that the practice of congressional chaplains was constitutional.[10]

Justice William Brennan dissented. The "unique history" of paid chaplains is not enough to make them constitutional, he argued.[11]

What about the armed forces? Without chaplains, many soldiers might not be able to practice their faith. For that reason, in 1985, a federal court of appeals said paid chaplains did not violate the Constitution.[12]

People in prison also have a right to practice their religion. States cannot force any prisoners to take part in services. They cannot discriminate among religions either. But they should give prisoners a reasonable chance to practice their faith. That can include paid chaplains, according to the Court.[13]

Displays of holiday decorations on public land have been the subject of contention. In response to protests, a sign was posted on this manger scene in Iowa stating that it was not sponsored or endorsed by the county.

Can government officially "bless" days of prayer? The country's first national Thanksgiving proclamation came in 1777. Thanksgiving became an official government holiday in 1863.[14] No one makes anyone pray on that day. And the holiday is not tied to any religion. Yet it implies that America is thanking someone—presumably God—for its blessings.

In the same vein, Congress passed a law for a National Day of Prayer in 1952. Since 1988, America has observed it on the first Thursday in May. Again, the day is not tied to any particular religion. No one is forced to pray.

Do days of prayer and thanksgiving cross over the line of neutrality? So far, these practices seem to be accepted.[15]

What about Sunday closing laws? The Supreme Court upheld such laws in 1961. In *McGowan* v. *Maryland*, Chief Justice Earl Warren agreed that the laws' initial goal was religious. They made sure people went to church. But times had changed. The laws' modern aim was "to provide a uniform day of rest for all citizens."[16]

Justice William Douglas disagreed. If Jewish or Muslim merchants observed their own Sabbath, they would have to close two days. They would lose money. Douglas noted, "The reverse side of an 'establishment' is a burden on the 'free exercise' of religion."[17]

Most Sunday closing laws are now gone. Discount stores, upscale department stores, malls, groceries, and other businesses now open on Sundays. Labor laws say businesses should make "reasonable accommodations" for their employees' religious needs. But employers do not have to make changes that cause undue hardship in doing business.[18]

"In God We Trust"

"In God We Trust" has appeared on U.S. coins since 1865. A similar phrase is in the fourth verse of "The Star-Spangled Banner." In 1956, a joint resolution of Congress made it America's national motto.[19]

As this book goes to press, the Supreme Court has not blessed the motto by holding it constitutional. But *dicta* in several cases suggest it would pass scrutiny.[20] *Dicta* are parts of an opinion that are not directly tied to a case's holding. They can be thought of as extra comments added by judges. While they are not binding, they tell about certain judges' opinions.

In 1977, *Wooley* v. *Maynard* said New Hampshire could not stop someone from covering up the motto on its license plates, "Live Free or Die." The motto went against George and Maxine Maynard's beliefs as Jehovah's Witnesses. The Court said the state could not make their car into a "mobile billboard" for its views.[21] In contrast, the Court said, printing the national motto on money did not make anyone advertise that view.

In 2001, a federal appeals court looked at Ohio's motto, "With God All Things Are Possible." The phrase is from the New Testament. Yet Ohio's lawyers said the state did not endorse Christianity. Rather, the words were a general message of hope. The Sixth Circuit held that the motto was constitutional.[22]

For now, it seems as if courts will approve of some references to God. But courts look at the questions closely. After all, the Pledge of Allegiance has been challenged in court. Future cases could raise more questions about religion in the public square.

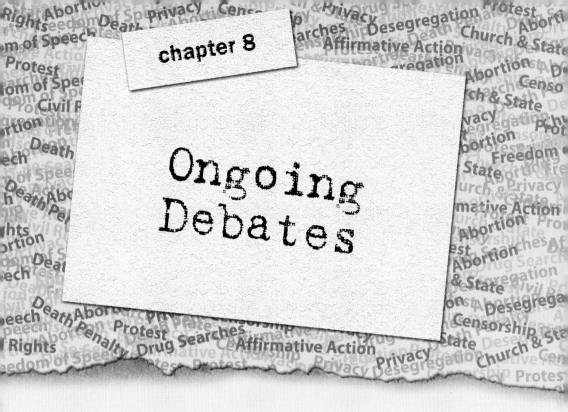

chapter 8

Ongoing Debates

No single case will end debate about church and state. Different groups will keep trying to redraw the lines.

This chapter looks at two areas where the debate will likely stay heated. One is school vouchers. The second issue deals with faith-based charities.

School Vouchers

In the 1990s, Cleveland's public schools were in big trouble. The schools met none of eighteen state standards. Only 10 percent of the students passed basic proficiency tests. Over two thirds of the high school students failed or dropped out before graduation. A federal court order put the city's schools under state control.

In response, the state adopted the Ohio Pilot Project Scholarship Program. Cleveland's low-income families had three choices. The program would pay for children to attend a private school or a public school in a nearby district. Children could go to publicly funded community schools or special magnet schools. Or, children could stay in their regular public schools and get tutoring.

From 1999 to 2000, 85 percent of private schools in the program were religious. Ninety-six percent of students in the scholarship program went to religious schools. The lower federal courts said the program was unconstitutional.

The case went to the Supreme Court. Dozens of groups on both sides filed *amicus curiae*, or "friend of the court," briefs. In 2002, *Zelman* v. *Simmons-Harris* held the Ohio program did not violate the Establishment Clause.[1] The Court split 5–4, with Justices Rehnquist, Antonin Scalia, Kennedy, Thomas, and O'Connor in favor of the program, and Justices Stevens, Souter, Stephen Breyer, and Ruth Bader Ginsburg against it.

Back in 1973, the Supreme Court struck down a state tax credit program to help parents pay for private religious schools.[2] The Ohio program was different, wrote Chief Justice William Rehnquist. The law in the 1973 case aimed to help religious schools. In contrast, Ohio's program was "entirely neutral with respect to religion."

It provides benefits directly to a wide spectrum of individuals, defined only by financial need and residence in a particular school district. It permits such individuals to exercise genuine choice among options public and private, secular and religious. . . . We hold that the program does not offend the Establishment Clause.[3]

Justice O'Connor agreed. Religious colleges, hospitals, and other groups got government funds on a neutral basis. Why not the schools? Besides, she wrote, the program satisfied the *Lemon* test. The goal was to help children, not religion. The range of options did not have the effect of promoting religion. And she saw no excessive entanglement of church and state.[4]

Justice Clarence Thomas also felt the program was constitutional. "Urban children have been forced into a system that continually fails them," he noted. The Ohio program "simply gives parents a greater choice as to where and in what manner to educate their children."[5]

Justice Stevens dissented:

Is a law that authorizes the use of public funds to pay for the indoctrination of thousands of grammar school children in particular religious faiths a "law respecting an establishment of religion" within the meaning of the First Amendment?[6]

His answer was yes. The families' other options did not matter to him.

Justice Souter noted that the program used

tax money to help teach religion. Some of those teachings went against other religious groups' views. No taxpayer should have to pay for that, he felt.[7]

Justice Breyer made a similar point. "The Court, in effect, turns the clock back," he wrote.[8] The risk of religious conflict worried him too.

Zelman opened the door for other tuition aid or "voucher" programs. When Congress looked at a program for the District of Columbia schools, it heard vigorous debate. Various groups argued that the programs promote parental choice. They also said children needed something better than the present schools.

Other groups objected. Some based their views on the Establishment Clause. Some school and teacher groups also argued that vouchers draw money away from troubled public schools. After heavy debate, Congress approved the D.C. program.[9]

Colorado adopted a program, but a court ruled it went against the state's constitution. In particular, it would limit school districts' control over locally raised money.[10] The debate continues in other states too. More court challenges may follow.

Faith-Based Initiatives

Can religious groups use public money to provide social services? The answer is yes—sometimes.

For years, religious groups have gotten public

money for social programs. But the programs could not be "pervasively religious." In other words, religion could not touch every part of the program. Often programs worked separately from other church activities.

Organizations could have a religious name. They could display a religious symbol like a cross or Star of David. But they could not require people to attend religious services in order to get help. And they could not discriminate on religion or race in giving help.

Public money has helped many groups run good programs. In 1996, for example, Catholic Charities USA got about $1.3 billion in public funds.[11] Lutheran Social Ministries, the Jewish Board of Family and Children's Services, and the Salvation Army have also used public funds to help people.

The 1988 case of *Bowen* v. *Kendrick* supports this.[12] A federal program let groups, including religious ones, get money to counsel teens about sexuality and pregnancy. Groups could not use grant money to help teens get abortions.

The Supreme Court found that the law had a secular purpose—reducing teen pregnancies. Yes, many religions feel premarital sex is wrong. Some religions object to abortion. But counseling was not religious *per se*. The grants were constitutional.

In 1996, Congress passed a Charitable Choice law.[13] People in public welfare programs could get some services from private groups. The government could not discriminate against religious groups in approving them to provide such services. The groups kept control over their organizations and beliefs. They could keep religious symbols and art on display. They could hire people whose beliefs matched their own.

But the programs still had to meet basic criteria. They could not discriminate against who got help. Preaching could not be part of the aid.

President George W. Bush wanted to make it even easier for faith-based groups to get money. He set up an Office of Faith-Based Initiatives in 2001.

In a 2002 speech, the President said his goal was to keep government from discriminating against religious groups. They should not have to "lose their mission or change their mission," he said. "We need to know that in our society, faith can move people in ways that government can't."[14]

Various civil liberties groups objected. "Pervasively religious" groups are suspect, says Steven Freeman at the Anti-Defamation League. He explains:

> Basically what they're saying to the person is you came to us for help, and the way we're going to help you is by helping you find religion. . . . I know that there are drug addiction programs where finding God has helped people conquer their addictions. But that's not something that taxpayer dollars should be funding.[15]

Consider the case of Joseph Hanas. After he pled guilty to marijuana possession, a Michigan court ordered the Catholic man to complete a Pentecostal Christian drug rehabilitation program. Hanas claimed the program would not give him drug treatment. Instead, it taught Pentecostal principles and urged him to abandon his faith. Hanas later sued after the court punished him for not finishing the program.[16] Critics worry that faith-based initiatives could use public money to fund such alleged abuses.

Jim Towey of the President's Office of Faith-Based Initiatives argued that the president's program would pass constitutional scrutiny. "You can't preach on Uncle Sam's dollar," he said.[17] But his comments implied that some faith groups might be more effective than others in social welfare programs. They also carried a veiled suggestion that pagan groups, like Wiccans, may not be as charitable as groups that believe in a single God.[18]

A lot of the debate focuses on hiring practices. The Charitable Choice law and President Bush's proposals said groups should be able to hire whomever they want. That way they would not have to change their mission.[19] After all, no one would make Planned Parenthood hire someone who felt that artificial contraception is wrong. Promoters of faith-based initiatives feel that religious groups deserve the same freedom. In practice, they say, that would mean hiring people from certain religions whose views mesh with theirs.

Critics like the American Civil Liberties Union object.[20] In general, the law forbids refusals to hire someone based on his or her race, age, religion, and gender. They agree that some church activities are exempt from the rule. But they do not feel public money should support any type of discrimination. If faith-based groups only want to hire people in certain categories, they say, let them do it on their own dollar. The same reasoning could apply to the 1996 Charitable Choice law too.

Debate about federal funding for faith-based charities will go on. No matter who sits in the White House, some politicians will seek more funds for religious charities. Also, the line between preaching and providing services is not always clear.

State programs will also draw scrutiny. In 2003, Florida's governor Jeb Bush announced that volunteers from religious groups would run rehabilitation programs at a state prison. Participation would be voluntary. How religious the programs would be was not clear.[21]

Ongoing Tensions

Debate will likely go on about other issues too: prayer in public schools, religious displays in public forums, and so on. After all, people care very

There are strict rules regarding the use of public money for religious groups that provide social services. Here a volunteer in a church soup kitchen passes out meals.

deeply about religion. "These issues have been around all of American history, and probably will continue to be around for the remainder of American history," notes Derek Davis at Baylor University.[22]

Learn all you can about issues of church and state. Informed opinions mean much more than gut reactions.

Be aware that your religious beliefs may color your opinions. Try to see things from other people's point of view. Understanding an issue means being able to see different sides.

"We can live together peacefully," says Davis. "We just need to make sure that we give people room to believe what they will and make sure that government doesn't interfere with that."[23]

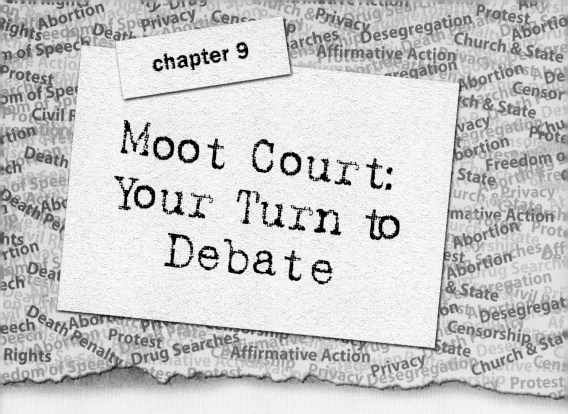

chapter 9

Moot Court: Your Turn to Debate

Law students use practice activities to develop courtroom skills. Mock trials are pretend trials. "Lawyers" present evidence, "witnesses" testify on the stand, "judges" make rulings, and "jurors" decide a case.

Moot court is pretend appellate court work. Students get the facts of a real or hypothetical (fictional) case and the trial court's ruling. They do research, write briefs, and argue legal issues before a make-believe panel of appeals court judges. The exercise hones research, writing, and debate skills.

Try a moot court activity with your class or club.[1] This activity deals with school vouchers. You can use the format to debate other legal issues too.

Step 1: Assign Roles

If your group has fewer than ten people, everyone can work on one set of briefs and arguments. If you have more than ten people, have several sets of teams. Here are the roles you will need to fill:

◇ Judges. If the group is large enough, have nine justices like the Supreme Court has. Otherwise, have a panel of three appellate court judges. Choose one person to be Chief Justice and direct the proceeding. The judges hear the attorneys' arguments, question them, and then write and deliver the final ruling. The court's majority opinion is the position agreed upon by a majority of the panel. Individual judges may choose to issue concurring or dissenting opinions of their own. Or if you can, invite three local lawyers to act as the judges.

◇ Two or more court clerks. They work with the judges to prepare five or more questions to ask the attorneys during oral arguments. Clerks also help with research for judges' opinions.

◇ A team of two or more attorneys for the appellant. They feel the lower court was wrong.

◇ A team of two or more attorneys for the appellee. They believe the lower court ruled correctly.

◇ Each team has a designated spokesperson to present the argument, but any of the attorneys can answer questions from the judges.

Attorneys must address the major issues by presenting the most persuasive arguments for their side.

◇ Two or more reporters. They interview the attorneys before the case and write news stories about the facts of the case and the final ruling.

◇ The bailiff, who calls the court to order. He or she will also time each side's oral argument.

Step 2: Prepare Your Case

Part 1: Gather Information

In 2002, *Zelman* v. *Simmons-Harris* upheld an Ohio school voucher program. But the Court was split. Six justices wrote opinions. Their views varied widely.

Zelman became legal precedent when it was decided. It became the law of the land on vouchers.

But the case was based on certain facts. A different program might not pass muster under the Court's reasoning. The makeup of the Court changes too, as justices retire. A new justice may be more likely to find fault in a voucher program. In rare cases, the Supreme Court even overrules one of its prior decisions.

Everyone in the moot court activity should look at the *Zelman* case. Your public library may have Supreme Court cases. The *Zelman* case is at 536 U.S. 639. That is volume 536 of *United States*

Reports. Start at page 639. If the library carries the *Supreme Court Reporter, Zelman* is at 122 S. Ct. 2460.

You may want to do more research on school vouchers too. Then review the facts of your moot court case.

George v. *Gracie*

The state of Gracie has a new voucher program. Its goal is to improve the quality of education. The law allows financial aid for any child in grades one through six who meets these criteria:

1. Family income is at or below the poverty level.
2. Average standardized test scores for the public school that the child would attend are below the 25th percentile for the state.

The child's parents have two choices:

Option A: The child stays in the public school and gets private or group tutoring. The state pays parents for all costs up to $1,000 a year, plus 50 percent of any amounts over that. The cap is $1,500 per student, per year.

Option B: The child can go to any private school or a public school in a nearby district. The state pays 100 percent of the tuition up to $1,000 per student. The family pays anything over that.

In the program's first year, half the qualifying children take the tutoring. The other half choose other schools. The state spends an average of $800 per student on tutoring.

Average tuition for students at other schools is $1,500. The state spends the full $1,000 per student for this option. About half the families make up the difference from their own funds. The other half get financial aid from the other schools. Religious groups run over two thirds of the schools chosen under Option B.

Other facts to know:

◇ The law setting up the program says it will end in six years.

◇ The state of Gracie already gives every public school in the state $2,000 for each student that attends. Thus, public schools lose money if students go elsewhere.

Assume that the George family has standing to challenge the program in federal court. The facts noted above come out at the trial. The court holds that the program does not violate the Establishment Clause. The George family has appealed.

Part 2: Write Your Briefs
A legal brief is a written presentation of your argument. Brainstorm with the lawyers on your team. How does the case compare to *Zelman* and other cases? How do the *Lemon* test factors apply? Which arguments are strongest for you? What are your weaknesses?

You may want to divide up arguments for research and writing. If so, be sure to work as a team to put the brief together. Otherwise, your brief may have holes or read poorly.

In real life, court rules spell out what briefs must have. Use these rules for your moot court activity:

1. The cover page should have the case name, *George* v. *Gracie*. Say whether it is for appellant or appellee. List the lawyers' names. (This page will not count for the page or word limit.)

2. The text of the brief should have these sections:

   A. Statement of the issue for review: What question is before the court?

   B. Statement of the case: What is this case about? How did the trial court rule?

   C. Statement of the facts: Briefly describe the facts relevant to the case.

   D. Summary of the argument: Sum up your argument in 150 words or less.

   E. Argument: Spell out the legal arguments that support your side. You can split this into sections with subheadings for each part. Include references to cases or authorities that help your side.

   F. Conclusion: Ask the court to rule for your client.

3. Real appeals briefs may be thirty pages long. Limit your brief to no more than five typed pages, double-spaced, or about 1,250 words. If possible, type on a computer. Otherwise, write *very* neatly.

4. On an agreed-upon date, each team gives the other side a copy of its brief. Each judge gets a copy too. If you do this in class, give the teacher a copy. Be sure each team member keeps a copy of the brief too.

In real life, lawyers often prepare reply briefs. They answer points made by the other side. You will not do that. But you should be ready to answer their points in oral argument.

Part 3: Prepare for Oral Argument

Judges should read all the briefs before oral argument. They should prepare questions for the lawyers.

Each side will have up to fifteen minutes to argue its case.

Step 3: Hold the Oral Argument

Part 1: Assemble the Participants

If your group is small, everyone can watch the oral argument. Otherwise, have the judges hear oral argument in a separate room. Have just one set of lawyers for each side present. That way, no one gets an unfair advantage.

> ◇ The judges sit together in the front of the room. This is the bench. They should not enter until the bailiff calls the court to order. A speaking podium or lectern faces the bench.

> ◇ The appellant's team of attorneys sits at one side, facing the judges.

◇ The appellee's team sits at the opposite side, also facing the judges.

◇ The reporters sit at the back.

◇ As the judges enter, the bailiff calls the court to order: "Oyez (oy-yay)! Oyez! Oyez! The _____ Court of the United States is now in session with the Honorable Chief Justice _____ presiding. All will stand and remain standing until the judges are seated and the Chief Justice has asked all present to be seated."

Part 2: Present the Case

◇ The Chief Justice calls the case and asks whether the parties are ready. Each team's spokesperson answers, "Yes."

◇ The appellant's spokesperson approaches the podium saying, "May it please the Court." Then argument begins. Judges interrupt when they wish to ask a question. The attorneys respectfully answer any questions as asked. Do not get flustered if a judge interrupts with a question. Answer the question honestly. Then move on.

◇ Then the appellee's team takes its turn.

◇ Each team has up to fifteen minutes to present its argument. If the appellant's team wants, it can save five minutes of its time to rebut the appellee's argument. If so, the spokesperson should inform the court before sitting down.

◇ After the arguments, the bailiff tells everyone to rise as the judges leave to debate their decision.

◇ At this time, reporters may interview lawyers for the parties and begin working on their articles.

Step 4: Publish and Report the Decision

After oral argument, the panel of judges decides who wins the case. A majority of the judges must agree on the outcome. If students act as the judges, they should write an opinion explaining their decision. If a judge disagrees, that person can write a dissent.

The total length of all the opinions should be under five double-spaced typed pages. (Real judges' opinions are often much longer, as *Zelman* shows.) Copies of the opinions should go to lawyers for both sides, plus the teacher.

If guest lawyers acted as judges, they do not have to write opinions. But ask them to tell your group what points persuaded them. They can also award certificates to teams for the best brief and for the best oral argument.

Reporters may interview the lawyers again, if they want to. Reporters' stories discussing the case and the outcome are due within twenty-four hours. Limit articles to five hundred words or less.

Questions for Discussion

1. Imagine being the only person in your town who practiced a certain faith. Are there activities at school or in your town that might make you uncomfortable?

2. *Are You There, God? It's Me, Margaret* was published in 1970. Religion is a main theme in this book by Judy Blume. Margaret's parents do not want to raise her as either Jewish or Catholic. Organized religion confuses Margaret. She talks to God in her own way.

   Imagine you are a sixth-grade reading teacher. You care about separation of church and state. Would you assign Blume's book? How would your lesson deal with the topic of religion?

   Suppose a public school holds a library week celebration. Students make posters about their favorite books. Nisha chooses Blume's book. Her poster shows the book cover and says, "You've got to talk to God." Should the school display Nisha's poster?

3. The National Gallery and other museums throughout the country receive money from the government. Their collections include many paintings and sculptures with religious themes. What arguments might someone make against

such government-sponsored displays? What arguments could someone make to say government should not exclude religious art from its support?

4. Daniel's public school kindergarten had a holiday party in December. The school let children pass out little gifts. One child passed out dreidels. Jewish children often play with these small tops at Hanukkah. The teacher allowed that. But the school balked when Daniel wanted to pass out candy canes with an attached religious story. What arguments would you make if you were the school's lawyer? What arguments would you make if you were Daniel's lawyer?

5. Christmas is a national holiday. Millions of Americans view it as a religious holy day. Other people do not celebrate it at all. Suppose someone sues to challenge whether Christmas can be a national holiday. What arguments would you make if you were that person's lawyer? What arguments would you make on the other side to keep Christmas as a national holiday? How do you think the Supreme Court would come out on the issue?

Chapter Notes

Chapter 1. One Nation Under God?

1. H.R. Rep. No. 83-1693, p. 3 (1954).

2. 100 Cong. Rec. 8618 (1954).

3. *Newdow* v. *U.S. Congress*, 328 F.3d 466, 488 (2002).

4. 328 F.3d 466, 493 (Fernandez, J., dissenting).

5. 319 U.S. 624, 642 (1943).

6. *Lipp* v. *Morris*, 579 F.2d 834 (3d Cir. 1978); *Goetz* v. *Ansell*, 477 F.2d 636 (2d Cir. 1973).

7. Public Law 107-293, 116 Stat. 2057 (Nov. 13, 2002).

8. *Newdow* v. *U.S. Congress*, 328 F.3d 466 (9th Cir., 2003).

9. Charles Lane, "Court Is Asked To Keep 'Under God' in Pledge," *Washington Post*, May 1, 2003, p. A7.

10. 980 F.2d 437 (7th Cir. 1992).

11. *Elk Grove Unified School District* v. *Newdow*, 124 S.Ct. 2301, 2307, 2310 (2004).

12. 124 S.Ct. 2301, 2312-33 (2004).

13. American Civil Liberties Union, "Religious Liberty," n.d., <http://www.aclu.org/ReligiousLiberty/ReligiousLibertyMain.cfm> (December 1, 2003).

14. Telephone interview with Derek Davis, Baylor University, J. M. Dawson Institute of Church-State Studies, December 15, 2003.

Chapter 2. Church and State in Early America

1. "The Maryland Act of Toleration," *University of Virginia Religious Freedom Homepage*, 2001, <http://religiousfreedom.lib.virginia.edu/sacred/md_toleration_1649.html> (October 6, 2004).

2. "Pennsylvania Charter of Privileges," October 28, 1701, in Henry Steele Commager and Milton Cantor, eds., *Documents of American History*, vol. 1 (Englewood Cliffs, N.J.: Prentice-Hall, 1988), pp. 40–41; Joseph E. Illick, *Colonial Pennsylvania: A History* (New York: Charles Scribner's Sons, 1976), p. 14.

3. Michael W. McConnell, "Establishment and Disestablishment at the Founding, Part I: Establishment of Religion," *William and Mary Law Review*, April 2003, pp. 2105, 2110–2112.

4. James Madison, "Memorial and Remonstrance Against Religious Assessments," *Annals of American History*, 1785, <http://america.eb.com/america/article?eu=410994> (January 8, 2004).

5. Robert S. Alley, *School Prayer: The Court, the Congress, and the First Amendment* (Buffalo, N.Y.: Prometheus Books, 1994), pp. 54–56; see also Philip Hamburger, *Separation of Church and State* (Cambridge, Mass.: Harvard University Press, 2002), p. 105.

6. Derek H. Davis, *Religion and The Continental Congress, 1774–1789: Contributions to Original Intent* (Oxford and New York: Oxford University Press, 2000), p. 210, quoting Washington's Farewell Address.

7. Charles F. Patterson, *The True Meaning of the Constitution: Ratifier Understanding* (Xenia, Ohio: Bentham Press, 2002), p. 213.

8. Davis, pp. 224–226.

9. *Torcaso* v. *Watkins*, 367 U.S. 488 (1961). See generally "Discrimination Because of Religious Creed in Respect of Appointment, Compensation, Etc., of Public Officers," 130 ALR 1516.

10. *McDaniel* v. *Paty*, 435 U.S. 618 (1978).

11. Hamburger, pp. 216–218; Robert S. Alley, *Without a Prayer: Religious Expression in Public Schools* (Amherst, N.Y.: Prometheus Books, 1996), p. 101, n. 25, and p. 227.

12. Hamburger, pp. 219–221; Thomas C. Berg, *The State and Religion in a Nutshell* (St. Paul, Minn.: West Group, 1998), pp. 203–204.

13. *Reynolds* v. *United States*, 98 U.S. 145, 167 (1878).

14. *Church of the Holy Trinity* v. *United States*, 143 U.S. 457, 471 (1892).

15. *Bradfield* v. *Roberts*, 175 U.S. 291 (1899).

Chapter 3. Arguments for Strict Separation

1. Telephone interview with Steven Freeman, Anti-Defamation League, December 2, 2003.

2. Telephone interview with Jeremy Leaming, Americans United for Separation of Church and State, December 5, 2003.

3. *Engel* v. *Vitale*, 370 U.S. 421, 432 (1962).

4. Freeman.

5. *Herdahl* v. *Pontotoc County School District*, 933 F. Supp. 582, 585 (N.D. Miss. 1996); Robert S. Alley, *Without a Prayer: Religious Expression in Public*

Schools (Amherst, N.Y.: Prometheus Books, 1996), pp. 187–190, 229.

6. Stephen M. Feldman, *Law & Religion: A Critical Anthology* (New York: New York University Press, 2000), p. 296.

7. *Zelman* v. *Simmons-Harris*, 536 U.S. 639, 686 (2002) (Stevens, J., dissenting).

8. Leaming.

9. *World Book Encyclopedia*, "United States," vol. 20, pp. 98, 114 (2003).

10. Edwin Gaustad and Philip Barlow, *New Historical Atlas of Religion in America* (New York: Oxford University Press, 2001), pp. 382–387; see also "Largest Religious Groups in the United States of America," and "Religious Bodies Which Are the Largest Church in One or More U.S. States, 1990," *Adherents.com*, 2002, updated January 6, 2003, <http://www.adherents.com/rel_USA.html> (December 6, 2003).

11. Norman Redlich, American Jewish Congress, Testimony before the Senate Committee on the Judiciary, September 16, 1982, quoted in Robert S. Alley, *School Prayer: The Court, the Congress, and the First Amendment* (Buffalo, N.Y.: Prometheus Books, 1994), pp. 253–255.

12. Freeman.

13. Joseph R. Duncan, Jr., "Privilege, Invisibility, and Religion: A Critique of the Privilege that Christianity Has Enjoyed in the United States," *Alabama Law Review*, Winter 2003, pp. 617, 627–628.

14. *Engel* v. *Vitale*, 370 U.S. 421, 431 (1962) (footnotes omitted).

15. Leaming.

16. Francis Graham Lee, *Church-State Relations* (Westport, Conn.: Greenwood Press, 2002), p. 4.

17. "Jefferson's Letter to the Danbury Baptists," January 1, 1802, <http://www.loc.gov/lcib/9806/danpre.html> (July 9, 2004).

18. "Largest Religious Groups in the United States of America."

19. Leaming.

20. Ibid.

21. *Everson* v. *Board of Education of Ewing Township*, 330 U.S. 1, 15 (1947).

Chapter 4. Arguments Against a Sharp Dividing Line

1. Telephone interview with John W. Whitehead, The Rutherford Institute, December 4, 2003.

2. Ibid.

3. Ibid.

4. *Board of Education of the Westside Community Schools* v. *Mergens*, 496 U.S. 226 (1990).

5. Whitehead.

6. *Zorach* v. *Clauson*, 343 U.S. 306, 313 (1952).

7. Charles F. Patterson, *The True Meaning of the Constitution: Ratifier Understanding* (Xenia, Ohio: Bentham Press, 2002), p. 212, quoting William Blackstone's *Commentaries on the Laws of England*.

8. U.S. Department of State, "The Northwest

Ordinance (1787)," Article 3, <http://usinfo.state.gov/usa/infousa/facts/democrac/5.htm> (July 22, 2004).

9. Thomas Nathan Peters, "Religion, Establishment, and the Northwest Ordinance: A Closer Look at an Accommodationist Argument," *Kentucky Law Journal*, Spring, 2000–2001, pp. 743, 746; see also Patterson, pp. 217–218.

10. Philip Hamburger, *Separation of Church and State* (Cambridge, Mass.: Harvard University Press, 2002), p. 71, quoting Rev. Timothy Stone of Connecticut, "A Sermon," 1792.

11. Edwin S. Gaustad, *Sworn on the Altar of God: A Religious Biography of Thomas Jefferson* (Grand Rapids, Mich.: William B. Eerdmans Publishing Company, 1996), pp. 157–180.

12. *Mitchell* v. *Helms*, 530 U.S. 793, 828 (2000); see also Krista Kafer, "School Choice in 2003: An Old Concept Gains New Life," *New York University Annual Survey of American Law*, 2003, pp. 439, 451–452; Francis Graham Lee, *Church-State Relations* (Westport, Conn.: Greenwood Press, 2002), p. 383.

13. *Everson* v. *Board of Education*, 330 U.S. 1, 18 (1947).

14. Hamburger, pp. 399–463.

15. *Board of Education* v. *Allen*, 392 U.S. 236, 251 (1968) (Black, J., dissenting).

16. Lee, p. 383.

17. Derek H. Davis, *Religion and The Continental Congress, 1774–1789: Contributions to Original Intent*

(Oxford and New York: Oxford University Press, 2000), p. 213.

18. Telephone interview with Derek Davis, Baylor University, J. M. Dawson Institute of Church-State Studies, December 15, 2003.

19. Robert S. Alley, *School Prayer: The Court, the Congress, and the First Amendment* (Buffalo, N.Y.: Prometheus Books, 1994), p. 124, quoting Graham; see also Stephen Strehle, *The Separation of Church and State: Has America Lost Its Moral Compass?* (Lafayette, La.: Huntington House Publishers, 2001), pp. 116–123, 134–135.

20. *Newdow v. United States Congress*, 328 F3d 466, 481–482 (O'Scannlain, J., dissenting).

21. *Everson v. Board of Education*, 330 U.S. 1, 18 (1947).

22. "Online Chat with Jim Towey," *Whitehouse.gov*, November 26, 2003, <http://www.whitehouse.gov/ask/20031126.html> (December 14, 2003).

Chapter 5. The Law of the Land

1. *Cantwell v. Connecticut*, 310 U.S. 296, 303 (1940).

2. 403 U.S. 602 (1971).

3. *Bowen v. Kendrick*, 487 U.S. 589, 615 (1988).

4. See, e.g., *Good News Club v. Milford Central School*, 533 U.S. 98 (2001); *Capitol Square Review and Advisory Board v. Pinette*, 515 U.S. 753, 767 (1995).

5. See, e.g., *Everson v. Board of Education*, 330 U.S. 1, 15–16 (1947); see also Thomas C. Berg, *The State and Religion in a Nutshell* (St. Paul, Minn.: West Group, 1998), pp. 31–34.

6. *Bob Jones University* v. *United States*, 461 U.S. 574 (1983); see also Steven P. Brown, *Trumping Religion: The New Christian Right, the Free Speech Clause, and the Courts* (Tuscaloosa: The University of Alabama Press, 2002), p. 22–23.

7. 397 U.S. 644, 675 (1970).

8. *Welsh* v. *United States*, 398 U.S. 333 (1970); *United States* v. *Seeger*, 380 U.S. 163 (1965); see also Darien A. McWhirter, *The Separation of Church and State* (Phoenix, Ariz.: Oryx Press, 1994), pp. 98–99.

9. *Wisconsin* v. *Yoder*, 406 U.S. 205 (1972).

10. *United States* v. *Lee*, 455 U.S. 252 (1982); Louis Fisher, *Religious Liberty in America: Political Safeguards* (Lawrence, Kans.: University Press of Kansas, 2002), pp. 214–215.

11. *Board of Education of Kiryas Joel Village School District v. Grumet*, 512 U.S. 687 (1994).

12. *Agostini* v. *Felton*, 521 U.S. 203 (1997).

13. *Church of the Lukumi Babalu Aye, Inc.,* v. *City of Hialeah*, 508 U.S. 520, 532 (1993).

14. *City of Boerne* v. *Flores*, 521 U.S. 507 (1997).

15. 456 U.S. 228 (1982).

16. 345 U.S. 67, 70 (1953).

17. *Larkin* v. *Grendel's Den, Inc.*, 459 U.S. 116 (1982).

18. 80 U.S. 679, 728 (1871); see also *Gonzalez* v. *Roman Catholic Church Archbishop of Manila*, 280 U.S. 1 (1929); Kent Greenawalt, "Hands Off! Civil Court Involvement in Conflicts over Religious Property," *Columbia Law Review*, 1998, p. 1843.

19. *Kedroff* v. *St. Nicholas Cathedral*, 344 U.S. 94 (1952).

20. *Serbian Eastern Orthodox Diocese* v. *Milivojevich*, 426 U.S. 696 (1976).

21. 443 U.S. 595, 602–604 (1979).

22. *Corporation of Presiding Bishop* v. *Amos*, 483 U.S. 327 (1987).

23. Fox Butterfield, "Report Details Sex Abuse by Priests and Inaction by a Diocese," *New York Times*, March 4, 2003, p. A16; Alan Cooperman and Lena H. Sun, "Hundreds of Priests Removed Since '60s," *Washington Post*, June 9, 2002, p. A1; Michael Paulson, "Pope Decries 'Sins' of Priests," *Boston Globe*, March 22, 2002, p. A1.

24. John S. Baker, Jr., "Prosecuting Dioceses and Bishops," *Boston College Law Review*, July–September 2003, p. 1061; Rev. John J. Coughlin, "The Clergy Sexual Abuse Crisis and the Spirit of Canon Law," *Boston College Law Review*, July–September 2003, p. 977; Wayne A. Logan, "Criminal Law Sanctuaries," *Harvard Civil Rights-Civil Liberties Law Review*, Summer 2003, p. 321; John H. Mansfield, "Constitutional Limits on the Liability of Churches for Negligent Supervision and Breach of Fiduciary Duty," *Boston College Law Review*, July–September 2003, p. 1167.

Chapter 6. Religion in the Schools

1. *Illinois ex rel. McCollum* v. *Board of Education*, 333 U.S. 203, 212 (1948).

2. *Zorach* v. *Clauson*, 343 U.S. 306 (1952).

3. *Engel* v. *Vitale*, 370 U.S. 421, 422 (1962).

4. Ibid.

5. *Abington School District* v. *Schempp*, 374 U.S. 203, 225 (1963).

6. 374 U.S. 203, 313 (1963) (Stewart, J., dissenting).

7. Robert S. Alley, *School Prayer: The Court, the Congress, and the First Amendment* (Buffalo, N.Y.: Prometheus Books, 1994), pp. 122, 123.

8. *Wallace* v. *Jaffree*, 472 U.S. 38, 59 (1985), citing *Lemon* v. *Kurtzman*, 403 U.S. 602 (1971).

9. 472 U.S. 38, 89 (1985).

10. *Brown* v. *Gwinnett County Schools*, 112 F.3d 1464 (11th Cir. 1997).

11. *Lee* v. *Weisman*, 505 U.S. 577, 592 (1992).

12. *Santa Fe Independent School District* v. *Doe*, 530 U.S. 290, 304–305, 309 (2000).

13. 20 U.S.C. §§ 4071-4074.

14. *Board of Education of the Westside Community Schools* v. *Mergens*, 496 U.S. 226, 250 (1990) (emphasis in original).

15. *Lamb's Chapel* v. *Center Moriches Union Free School District*, 508 U.S. 384 (1993).

16. 515 U.S. 819 (1995).

17. *Widmar* v. *Vincent*, 454 U.S. 263 (1981).

18. *Good News Club* v. *Milford Central School*, 533 U.S. 98, 110 (2001); see also Ashley Myrick, "How Can the Church Get Fit if the Fifth Circuit Won't Let It Exercise?" *Baylor Law Review*, Spring 2002, p. 449.

19. *Illinois* ex rel. *McCollum* v. *Board of Education*, 333 U.S. 203 (1948).

20. 154 Tenn. 105, 121, 289 S.W. 363, 367 (1927).

21. 393 U.S. 97, 106 (1968).

22. 482 U.S. 578 (1987).

23. *Freiler* v. *Tangipahoa Parish Board of Educ.*, 185 F.3d 337 (1999), cert. denied 530 U.S. 1251 (2000).

24. Mike Lafferty, "Proposed Lesson on Evolution Upsets Scientists," *Columbus Dispatch*, December 4, 2003, p. 8C; Scott Stephens, "Science Standards Debate Continues Evolving in Ohio," *Cleveland Plain Dealer*, November 27, 2003, p. B4; Judith Nygren, "Science Standards Challenged," *Omaha World Herald*, May 10, 2002, p. 5B.

25. *Altman* v. *Bedford Central School District*, 245 F.3d 49 (2d Cir. 2001).

26. Telephone interview with Stephen Freeman, Anti-Defamation League, December 2, 2003.

27. *Board of Education* v. *Allen*, 392 U.S. 236 (1968); *Cochran* v. *Louisiana*, 281 U.S. 370 (1930).

28. 330 U.S. 1 (1947).

29. 403 U.S. 602 (1971).

30. Ibid. at 625.

31. *Tilton* v. *Richardson*, 403 U.S. 672, 685-86 (1971).

32. *Committee for Pub. Educ. & Religious Liberty* v. *Nyquist*, 413 U.S. 756 (1973).

33. *Wolman* v. *Walter*, 433 U.S. 229 (1977).

34. 463 U.S. 388 (1983).

35. 509 U.S. 1 (1993).

36. 521 U.S. 203 (1997).

37. 530 U.S. 793 (2000).

38. 536 U.S. 639 (2002).

39. *Roemer v. Board of Public Works of Maryland*, 426 U.S. 736 (1976); *Hunt v. McNair*, 413 U.S. 734 (1973); *Tilton v. Richardson*, 403 U.S. 672 (1971).

40. 474 U.S. 481 (1986).

41. 124 S.Ct. 1307 (2004).

Chapter 7. Religion in the Public Square

1. *Glassroth v. Moore*, 335 F.3d 1282 (11th Cir. 2003); and John Johnson, "Panel Removes Alabama's 'Ten Commandments Judge,'" *Los Angeles Times*, November 14, 2003, p. A1; "Judicial Courage in Alabama," *New York Times*, November 14, 2003, p. A28.

2. *Stone v. Graham*, 449 U.S. 39, 41 (1980) (*per curiam*).

3. See, e.g., *McCreary County v. American Civil Liberties Union of Kentucky*, Case 03-1693, 2004 U.S. LEXIS 6693 (Oct. 12, 2004); *Orden v. Perry*, Case 03-1500, 2004 U.S. LEXIS 6691 (Oct. 12, 2004).

4. *Lynch v. Donnelly*, 465 U.S. 668, 681 (1984); Albert J. Menendez, *The December Wars: Religious Symbols and Ceremonies in the Public Square* (Buffalo, N.Y.: Prometheus Books, 1993), pp. 108–110, 113–117.

5. *Lynch v. Donnelly*, 465 U.S. 668, 711–712 (1984) (Brennan, J., dissenting). See also 465 U.S. at 727 (Blackmun, J., dissenting).

6. *County of Allegheny v. American Civil Liberties Union*, 492 U.S. 573 (1989); see also Menendez, pp.120–126.

7. *Capitol Square Review and Advisory Board* v. *Pinette*, 515 U.S. 753, 767 (1995).

8. Compare Menendez, pp. 122, 157, with *Calvary Chapel Church* v. *Broward County*, 299 F.Supp.2d 1295 (S.D. Fla. 2003).

9. *Marsh* v. *Chambers*, 463 U.S. 783, 788 (1983).

10. Ibid., n. 10.

11. Ibid. at 795, 803–804 (Brennan, J., dissenting).

12. *Katcoff* v. *Marsh*, 755 F.2d 223 (2d Cir. 1985).

13. See, e.g., *Cruz* v. *Beto*, 405 U.S. 319 (1972).

14. Derek H. Davis, *Religion and the Continental Congress, 1774–1789: Contributions to Original Intent* (Oxford and New York: Oxford University Press, 2000), pp. 84–87.

15. *Lynch* v. *Donnelly*, 465 U.S. 668, 675–676 (1984).

16. *McGowan* v. *Maryland*, 366 U.S. 420, 445 (1961).

17. Ibid. at 578 (1961) (Douglas, J., dissenting).

18. See Louis Fisher, *Religious Liberty in America: Political Safeguards* (Lawrence, Kans.: University Press of Kansas, 2002), pp. 218, 228–229. Compare *Frazee* v. *Illinois Employment Security Department*, 489 U.S. 829 (1989), with *Thornton* v. *Caldor*, 472 U.S. 703 (1985).

19. *Engel* v. *Vitale*, 370 U.S. 421, 440 n. 5 (1962) (Douglas, J., concurring).

20. *Elk Grove Unified School District* v. *Newdow*, 124 S.Ct. 2301, 2312, 2318–2319 (2004) (Rehnquist, J., concurring); *County of Allegheny* v. *American Civil Liberties Union*, 492 U.S. 573, 602 (1989); *Wooley* v.

Maynard, 430 U.S. 705, 717 n. 15 (1977); *Lynch* v. *Donnelly*, 465 U.S. 668, 676 (1984); *Engel* v. *Vitale*, 370 U.S. 421, 449–450 (1962) (Stewart, J., dissenting).

21. *Wooley* v. *Maynard*, 430 U.S. 705, 715 (1977).

22. *ACLU* v. *Capitol Square Review & Advisory Board*, 243 F.3d 289 (6th Cir. 2001) (*en banc*); Richard F. Suhrheinrich and T. Melindah Bush, "The Ohio Motto Survives the Establishment Clause," *Ohio State Law Journal*, 2003, p. 585.

Chapter 8. Ongoing Debates

1. *Zelman* v. *Simmons-Harris*, 536 U.S. 639 (2002).

2. *Committee for Public Ed. & Religious Liberty* v. *Nyquist*, 413 U.S. 756 (1973).

3. *Zelman* v. *Simmons-Harris*, 536 U.S. 639, 662–63 (2002).

4. 536 U.S. 668–676 (O'Connor, J., concurring).

5. 536 U.S. at 676, 680 (Thomas, J., concurring).

6. 536 U.S. at 684 (Stevens, J., dissenting).

7. 536 U.S. at 716 (Souter, J., dissenting).

8. 536 U.S. at 728 (Breyer, J., dissenting).

9. Jay Mathews, "Voucher Holders Shop Schools," *Washington Post*, June 23, 2004, p. B1; Spencer S. Hsu and Justin Blum, "D.C. School Vouchers Win Final Approval," *Washington Post*, January 23, 2004, p. A1.

10. Mindy Sink, "National Briefing—Rockies: Colorado: Voucher Law Unconstitutional," *New York Times*, June 29, 2004, p. A22; *Owens* v. *Colorado Cong. of Parents*, Supreme Court of Colorado, Case 03SA364,

June 28, 2004, <http://www.courts.state.co.us/supct/opinions/2003/03SA364.doc> (July 26, 2004).

11. Steven K. Green, "Charitable Choice and Neutrality Theory," *New York University Annual Survey of American Law*, 2000, pp. 33, 36; see also Stephen V. Monsma, *The "Pervasively Sectarian" Standard in Theory and Practice*, Notre Dame J.L. Ethics & Pub. Policy, 1999, pp. 321, 322–323.

12. *Bowen* v. *Kendrick*, 487 U.S. 589 (1988).

13. 42 United States Code, Section 604a. See Thomas C. Berg, *The State and Religion in a Nutshell* (St. Paul, Minn.: West Group, 1998), pp. 221–222.

14. Office of the White House, "President Promotes Faith-Based Initiative," April 11, 2002, <http://www.whitehouse.gov/news/releases/2002/04/20020411-5.html> (April 13, 2002).

15. Telephone interview with Steven Freeman, Anti-Defamation League, December 2, 2003.

16. American Civil Liberties Union, "Michigan Court Punishes Catholic Man for Refusing Conversion to Pentecostal Faith in Drug Rehab Program," press release, July 20, 2004, <http://www.aclu.org/ReligiousLiberty/ReligiousLiberty.cfm?ID=16138&c=142> (July 23, 2004).

17. "Online Chat with Jim Towey," *Whitehouse.gov*, November 26, 2003, <http://www.whitehouse.gov/ask/20031126.html> (December 14, 2003).

18. See Alan Cooperman, "White House Aide Angers Pagans," *Washington Post*, December 7, 2003, p. A23.

19. "Online Chat with Jim Towey."

20. American Civil Liberties Union, "ACLU of Louisiana Opposes Renewed White House Push for Taxpayer Funded Religious Discrimination," press release, January 15, 2004, <http://www.aclu.org/ReligiousLiberty/ReligiousLiberty.cfm?ID=14737&c=29> (January 21, 2004).

21. Paul Pinkham, "Lawtey to House Nation's First Faith-Based Prison," *Florida Times-Union*, December 6, 2003, <http://www.jacksonville.com/tu-online/stories/120603/met_14232359.shtml> (December 14, 2003).

22. Telephone interview with Derek Davis, Baylor University, J. M. Dawson Institute of Church-State Studies, December 15, 2003.

23. Ibid.

Chapter 9. Moot Court: Your Turn to Debate

1. Adapted from Millie Aulbur, "Constitutional Issues and Teenagers," *The Missouri Bar*, n.d., <http://www. mobar.org/teach/clesson.htm> (December 10, 2004); Street Law, Inc. and The Supreme Court Historical Society, "Moot Court Activity," 2002, <http://www.landmarkcases.org/mootcourt.html> (December 10, 2004); with suggestions from Ron Fridell.

Glossary

accommodationists—People who do not want strict separation of church and state but feel government can help, or accommodate, people in the free exercise of their religion.

agnostic—Someone who takes no position on whether there is a god.

atheist—Someone who denies that there is a god.

coercion—Force, compulsion, or intimidation.

Establishment Clause—Part of the First Amendment that says Congress shall make no law respecting an establishment of religion.

Free Exercise Clause—Part of the First Amendment that says Congress shall make no law limiting the free exercise of religion.

nondenominational—Not specific to any one religious group, even if there is a general religious tone.

nonsectarian—Not belonging to or limited to any specific religion.

sectarian—Related to a religious group.

secular—Not having to do with religion. Secularism is a focus on worldly things, without religion.

theocracy—Church-led government.

Further Reading

Djupe, Paul A., and Laura R. Olson. *Encyclopedia of American Religion and Politics*. New York: Facts on File, 2003.

Dudley, William, ed. *Religion in America: Opposing Viewpoints*. San Diego, Greenhaven Press, 2002.

Farish, Leah. *Lemon v. Kurtzman: The Religion and Public Funds Case*. Berkeley Heights, N.J.: Enslow Publishers, 2000.

Gaustad, Edwin S. *Church and State in America*. New York: Oxford University Press, 2003.

Loren, Julia C. *Engel v. Vitale: Prayer in the Public Schools*. San Diego: Lucent Books, 2001.

Marzilli, Alan. *Religion in Public Schools*. Philadelphia: Chelsea House, 2004.

Internet Addresses

American Civil Liberties Union "Religious Liberty" Home Page

<http://www.aclu.org/ReligiousLiberty/Religious LibertyMain.cfm>

Baylor University, J.M. Dawson Institute of Church-State Studies

<http://www3.baylor.edu/Church_State>

The Rutherford Institute, "Religious Freedom"

<http://www.rutherford.org/issues/religious_ freedom.asp>

Index